The Wr

Book

About the authors

Amy Brown

Amy is a professor of public health based in the School of Health and Social Care at Swansea University in the UK. With a background in psychology, her research explores experiences of pregnancy, birth and early parenting with a particular focus on supporting infant feeding and mental health.

Amy is a respected international speaker and has published over 100 research papers, many of which underpin policy and practice guidelines including in the UK, Australia and USA. She is the author of ten books including *Breastfeeding Uncovered* (2016; 2021), *Informed is Best* (2019) and *Covid Babies* (2021).

Lyndsey Hookway

Lyndsey is an experienced paediatric nurse, children's public health nurse, IBCLC, responsive sleep and parenting advocate, and PhD student. Her current focus is on teaching, speaking, research and writing, alongside her support and advocacy for parents of breastfed medically complex children.

Lyndsey is a respected international speaker and author of *Holistic Sleep Coaching: Gentle Alternatives to Sleep Training for Health and Childcare Professionals (2018), Let's talk about your new family's sleep (2020), Still Awake (2021)* and *Breastfeeding the Brave* - due for publication in 2022.

The Writing Book

How to plan, write and publish your work

Amy Brown & Lyndsey Hookway

TR Books

The Writing Book: How to plan, write and publish your work
First published in the UK by Thought Rebellion Limited 2022

ISBN 978-1-7396929-0-2

Also available as an ebook

Proofread and indexed by Jules Wraith

Cover design: Leanne Pearce

A catalogue record for this book is available from the British Library.

Contents

Introduction

Welcome to the wonderful world of writing. We're so glad you're here to invest in your writing – whether you are just getting started, changing tack or you want to get *even* better. We want to help you explore all your reasons for writing, understand your audience, and help you hone your idea into a marketable and successful book. More than this, we want to help you to become an *even* better writer. We don't want to leave it there though. We also want you to enjoy the process, and develop as a person, growing in confidence and learning new skills too.

There are lots of books on the market that cover how to write and publish your work, so why is this one any different? Well, this book covers all the important aspects of developing your writing, specifically for nonfiction books. However, it goes much further than that, drawing on our varied experiences of writing and presenting our work, to support you with all the additional skills we feel are so important to being a successful writer, yet are often missing from 'how to write' books. With this in mind we have included chapters on the psychology of writing (battling impostor syndrome, dealing with rejection and facing up to criticism) and successful promotion and dissemination via the conference scene and social media.

Who are we and how did we end up writing this book?

Amy is a professor of maternal and child health with almost twenty years' experience of supporting university students from around the world with their research and writing across the fields of public health, psychology and childhood development. Her expertise is in early parenting, particularly infant feeding, infant growth and development, and mental health. Like many, Amy became fascinated in her research subject after having her first baby and realising that there was a large gap in terms of putting evidence-based care into practice. She wanted to undertake the research that mattered to families and disseminate it in a way that was useful to them.

In meeting this aim she has now published over 100 peer-reviewed research papers and chapters in edited collections as well as ten books. Amy writes widely, on her website **(www.professoramybrown.co.uk)** and for the media. She has collaborated widely with the media in bringing research to life and has featured in multiple newspapers, on radio shows and television documentaries. She is passionate about creating and disseminating knowledge and coaching others to do so.

Lyndsey has a very different background to Amy, and is the clinician of the two. With twenty years' experience as a paediatric nurse, public health nurse (health visitor), IBCLC, and sleep coach, she has mostly offered families practical and clinical support. She has worked in the NHS, on paediatric wards, paediatric high dependency, NICU, clinics and the community, as well as in private practice, and voluntarily in Malaysia, and Kenya. Her second daughter became profoundly unwell and forced a resignation from clinical practice in 2017, but every cloud has a silver lining, and she threw herself into writing, teaching and speaking instead. She has written for many newspapers, magazines, several chapter segments, and contributed to NICE guidelines.

Lyndsey also maintains a busy social media presence and blogs at her website **(www.lyndseyhookway.com)**. After many years of evidence-based practice, she found a love for writing books and is now firmly addicted with three published and two more in the pipeline. In her spare time she is undertaking a PhD but she continues to write, teach an international online program, and speak for various organisations. For the last five years she has been constantly writing, and feels slightly bereft if she's not plotting a new book.

We both speak to audiences all over the world about responsive infant feeding, sleep, early parenting, attachment, hospitalisation and mental health. This is where our expertise lies, and therefore what we tend to write about, teach and research. However, whether your expertise is in marine biology or astrology, as long as we're talking nonfiction you will get a huge amount out of this book, as we have written it to be as applicable as possible, in a non genre-specific way.

Why we wrote this book

Personally, we think books are wonderful, and hopefully that's why you're here too. We're fans of kindle and audiobooks too, but there's just something about a physical book that (in our humble opinion) is a bit special. Books have been around for thousands of years, yet despite all the innovation that could have made the simple pleasure of reading a book obsolete, the appeal of a new book endures. People will always want books. They make perfect gifts, and they are available on every conceivable topic, and some *in*conceivable ones too. Whatever project you are engaged with there is likely to be a book available. This could make it hard to keep generating new material, but of course books go out of date so there is a constant need to keep publishing.

Authors write books about subjects that fascinate, inspire, baffle and entertain their readers. Some authors write about the same topic their entire career, while others write multiple books about different topics. It's likely that even before you picked up this book you had a concept in mind to write about. The reason you want to write about your subject is probably first and foremost because you want more people to know what you know and to benefit from that knowledge. But there may be other secondary reasons for writing that might include personal accomplishment, the cathartic nature of writing about important topics, or simply a love of creating and the craft of writing.

It's no surprise then that so many people want to be part of such an appealing and enduring industry. Add to this the draw of sharing something that you're passionate and learned about, as well as the honour of being published, and it's easy to see why thousands of people every year choose to embark on the business of writing a book.

Personally, we wanted to write this book to support others in their journey to becoming writers or honing their writing skills. On a simple level we both love the experience of writing and crafting books. Our books are designed to support others within a specific aspect of their lives, whether that is supporting new parents, health professionals or policy makers to understand research and evidence and what that means on a practical level. After writing fifteen books between us, we felt that we wanted to share our experiences of what we have learned along the way, including the good, the bad and the ugly!

We also realised that people who want to write and promote their work tend to have a lot of the same questions and concerns. When compiling the structure of this book we wanted to add all the different questions we are both regularly asked, focussing on writing but also the broader experience of publishing, promoting and responding to criticisms of your work. We believe book writing is as much psychological as it is about writing skills, so we have included plenty of information and support about the areas that tend to give many authors a headache.

You might wonder if you belong here, or speculate about why certain people become writers while others do not? Rest assured that these are common emotions and something we very much cover in this book. We want to encourage you in your writing and re-establish the old-fashioned pride in being a writer. If you take writing seriously, you're in the right place. Are you the finished article yet? Probably not, and we'll let you into a secret – neither are we. Part of growing as a writer is accepting that it is a lifelong journey. Even when you have multiple publications under your belt there is still so much to learn and be curious about.

It wouldn't be unreasonable if your next thought is – 'Can *everyone* be a writer?' It was the influential and sharp-tongued journalist Christopher Hitchens who famously said, "Everybody *does* have a book in them, but in most cases that's where it should stay." He meant of course, to acknowledge that of the thousands of books out there, very few end up as bestsellers. Ouch!

However, 'becoming a bestseller' isn't always the goal of everyone who sits down to write. Realistically, few of us will become bestsellers but that doesn't mean our books are not worth crafting or the journey not worth experiencing. You might be aiming to build a career out of writing or you might simply be enjoying the process as a hobby. Maybe you plan to write lots of books, or maybe this will be your one and only. Both (and everything in between) are laudable goals and supporting you in meeting your own personal goals is the central reason for why we wrote this book.

Perhaps a better question than '*can everyone be a writer*?' is '*can anyone who has determination, drive and dedication be a writer?*' We think the answer to that question is – yes. But we also think that there is a difference between simply putting words down on paper and becoming a good writer. By 'good' we mean producing work that appeals to others but also being the best possible writer that you can be for yourself.

What makes a good writer?

So what makes a good writer, and how do you know whether your book is one that needs to be read on a mass scale? It is likely that everyone has a slightly different opinion on this, but we suggest the following six characteristics of a good writer:

1. **Fastidiousness:** to be a great writer with a book that doesn't end up on the slush pile, you'll need to be careful and observant about details. This is not just about grammatical and typographical errors, but also factual inaccuracies or sweeping statements. This is especially true in the nonfiction sector – for obvious reasons.

2. **Commitment:** you will need to be committed to your subject, but also to the writing process. Writing a book is hard work, and can feel relentless. It's not just writing it, but the edits, re-writes, proofreading, and getting it done even when you don't feel like it.

3. **Clear communication:** one of the fine arts of writing is coming up with clear and concise ways to explain complex concepts. Some of the most profound statements sound incredibly simple, but are the distillation of years of thought and study. A great writer infuses their writing with these nuggets of wisdom to explain something complicated and to make it accessible. Clear communication is also about writing that keeps the reader hooked.

4. **Vocabulary tailored to your intended audience:** there are many different styles of writing and many different audiences. The key is matching your approach to the needs of your readers. Sometimes your work may need to be read in a highly scientific way and at other times it needs to be simplified for readers who may be experiencing distress or confusion; for example we both have written research driven publications but also have books aimed at exhausted new parents. It is not necessarily about knowing all the 'big words', but matching your vocabulary to those who are likely to read your book.

5. **Love of reading:** to be a truly great writer, you really do have to love reading. Not only will you have to read your own work – sometimes multiple times, and to the point where you are sick of your manuscript, but you should be reading other work too. This is necessary in nonfiction as part of the research and background reading, but also - reading *any* kind of book will broaden your vocabulary and support your writing.

6. **Growth mindset:** coined by Carol Dweck, this is the concept that if we accept that we are works in progress, and our success is not something that is fixed, we can continue to grow and improve. Having this attitude means that we not only understand that we are never *finished* with the work of improvement, but also that with perseverance and learning, it is realistic and achievable to keep getting *even* better.

As you read through that list of characteristics, you will probably be able to identify with some of these already. However, maybe you're unsure about some of the others or are worried you might not be able to achieve them. Doubts are such a normal part of the process of writing but this is where we hope our book will help you - both in developing your skills and banishing the nagging voice of self-doubt! We believe *everyone* can improve their writing. Whether you're just starting out, have received multiple rejections, or you already have a couple of books to your name, we want to help you get even better.

How to use this book

We've covered four main themes in this book: developing your writing skills and focus, publishers and contracts, psychological aspects of writing, and promoting your work. You can certainly read it in chronological chapter order, but we also hope it serves as a resource for you to dip in and out of during the process of writing your first book and beyond. Certain chapters such as dealing with criticism or social media might be chapters that you come back to time and time again. We hope it is a supportive companion to you across your writing journey.

Our hope for you is that this book encourages you to grow and develop your writing skills. The way you approach and think about writing is so much more than just getting words down on the page. We'd love to see more and more excellent, high-quality books that have stretched and developed their authors and made a difference to their readers. For thousands of years, books have inspired, informed and gripped readers in thousands of disparate subjects and topics. We hope that through growing in confidence as a writer, your books become part of the solution to someone's knowledge gap.

Chapter 1

Why write a book?

Let's start at the very beginning. What's *really* involved in writing a book? If you close your eyes and imagine yourself a writer, what do you see?

Many people start off their writing journey with a vision of a log cabin in the woods reminiscent of the hugely successful and introverted one-time novelist J. D. Salinger. If you've watched the movie *Rebel in the Rye*, (which we highly recommend) you may insert yourself into Nicholas Hoult's character and feel slightly mis-sold that the reality of writing is typically not cocktail hours, world book tours and a bespoke writing hut. We've come a long way from the days of the typewriter and submitting a physical sheaf of papers to an editor in a smoke-filled publishing office, but we admit, parts of the process are now less romantic. There's perhaps less thrill and more anticlimax when you click 'send' on your final manuscript submission compared with handing over a wodge of carefully bound paper. But on the plus side, at least you won't risk soaking them all in a lake like Colin Firth's character in the film *Love Actually*.

We think that a lot of what appeals so much about this vision is not necessarily the log cabin or sepia lens of times gone by, but rather what it signalled. The importance, value, and dedicated time for writing. The brilliance of a character who comes good after often being so very misunderstood. And of course, triumph over adversity and recognition of what you have achieved. When our vision of writing books is tied up in this image it is about our hopes and dreams for the success of our book and our lives as a writer.

Rest assured, that sense of achievement is still possible, but realistically the process may look a little different. You absolutely can still feel that sense of achievement from collecting your thoughts in a coherent way so that others can benefit or be inspired... but the process may more likely have involved some snatched time in between feeding the kids or other deadlines from work, at least to start with. To keep you on track and to prevent disillusionment, we think it's only fair that aspiring, improving and established authors alike have realistic expectations about the writing process, as well as a clear sense that they are writing for the right reasons.

Benefits of writing for others

Let's start with perhaps the most important reason for writing a book – for the benefit of others. A book can articulate an argument, tell a story, summarise the evidence. But ultimately, writing for others is about conveying something to an audience that is of value and use to them. You have so much opportunity to use your knowledge, words and writing skills to make a real difference to people's lives.

Based on this, like it or not, whatever your reasons for writing your book, you are ultimately writing for, and will be judged by, others. Your words, and the meaning of your words will be public property. That means that you ought to consider your audience carefully as you write. The difference between writing a diary and a book is that your articulated thoughts will become public. And the difference between writing a blog, typically read by your friends, acquaintances and loyal followers, and a book is that the latter will reach new audiences.

We find it helps to consider who will read your book in a very conscious way as you write. Constantly check with yourself whether your words will make sense outside your brain where you have the benefit of context. Have you explained everything fully for someone who may not have any experience with your topic? We'll come back to this later as stepping outside your brain is a really challenging part of writing, especially when you live and breathe your subject.

You also have to consider that people have *paid money* to read your words. Make it worth their while! Because you are writing for others - your work will be judged and critiqued - which is why it's so nerve-wracking. People do not just want to learn information – they want to *enjoy* learning that information, and retain it. We help them by making sure our writing is clear, well-phrased, grammatically correct and has a logical flow. A sensitivity check is also important. How might people interpret your words? As supportive? Challenging? Empathetic? None of those are right or wrong per se, but they may affect how your words are received - and the assumptions that are made about your beliefs.

By always considering your reader the reviews will come and everyone will be raving about your book; which will, in turn, increase its reach. You will have the triple benefit of knowing you have helped others by writing something useful, that your work is well crafted, and that it is being shared and appreciated. Definitely author core goals!

What's in it for you?

If we're entirely honest with ourselves though, writing is about more than the benefit to others. There has to be something in it for *you* as well. From time to time, we all need to evaluate or re-evaluate what we're writing for especially if it takes us away from other parts of our lives. We've already touched on the satisfaction of helping others but what other benefits can writing bring?

Consider for a moment why you want to write a book. Perhaps you have a clear vision already and you bought this book to help you bring it to fruition. Or maybe you have a loose idea and you are hoping that reading this will sharpen your focus. You might just want to improve your writing of blogs, articles and social media posts. The chances are, that whatever it is you're writing, or considering writing, it is something you feel strongly about. It's rare to find someone who writes about something they have no interest in.

We'll take it as read that you love your subject. You might want to write to inspire others to love that which you are passionate about, or even reignite your own passion for your subject, writing or communicating. You might have a point to make, or a bone to pick. You might want to educate or inform. You might want to present your argument and make a solid case for a cause you believe in. Perhaps you love writing or teaching and the book you plan to publish is a natural progression of that. Maybe you're expected to write due to your profile or position. Maybe you want to leave a lasting legacy and be known as the person who wrote X. Maybe you're retiring, or stepping back and want to ensure that your knowledge is passed on.

Or maybe this is about deepening your own knowledge and developing your writing skills for your own pleasure. Some people write to immerse themselves more fully in a subject that they love. In having to research and plan your book you will learn more about your area. In writing, sometimes the secondary benefit is that you also learn about yourself. You will learn about your ability, your concentration, and how your mind works. Writing might be thought of as a personal challenge, target or goal. You'll also become frustrated with yourself, which will force you to learn ways to improve your focus and become more efficient. There will be a point where you want to give up and there is a certain pleasure in overcoming that.

We're just going to say it: Some people write for fame or to feel like a success. It's ok to acknowledge that you like the idea of being known for your subject, and certainly a book can be a good way to make yourself known. If *you* don't write the book, perhaps someone *else* will, and become well-known for it – which might feel frustrating. We would just advise caution with this particular personal aim though, as it's the one most likely to disappoint. Most authors do not become famous or sell millions of copies of books. Many will have success within a specific circle of interested colleagues and fans but it's unlikely to make you an internet sensation or put your face on the side of a bus. This doesn't mean that your work isn't important and needed - it's just about contextualising what you think success looks like.

Additionally, if you don't feel enough *without* your book, you may not feel enough with it either. Relying on *things* to fulfil us is a risky strategy. And if you have perfectionist tendencies, which we will talk about later in the book, you might find that as soon as you've written one book you'll just discover that you need to write another to feel successful. And another. And so on - this is where madness lies. Write for your audience, to make a difference, and to meet personal goals, but don't pin your hopes on being a global bestseller. There's so much more value in the former reasons (although fame and fortune would be nice). Ok, we're done. Author therapy is over for today.

Finally, we know you're thinking it, and wondering when we're going to say it – you might want to write for the money. Perhaps you're fed up with providing information for free, or blogging and churning out great tips and advice that goes viral. Maybe one day you just realised 'hey, if that had been a book instead of a blog, I could be off on a cruise by now'. You will certainly be paid for your writing. How *much* will depend on numerous factors – including who publishes your work, any advance you receive, the agreed royalty fee, and of course, how many copies you sell. Often more money comes from promoting your book, such as being asked to give a paid presentation or lead a workshop, than from actual book sales.

In general, larger publishing houses may mean a bigger advance, and a bigger budget for marketing and promoting your book – which clearly will increase the sales and therefore your royalties. However, for your work to be picked up by a major publisher, you'll either have to have a killer book proposal that an agent loves and can sell to the publisher, or be an established author or public figure. A little luck sometimes helps as well of course. Royalties (which sound lovely don't they!?) are generally about 8 - 10% of the recommended retail price of the book depending on the format and publisher. So if your book's RRP is £10, conservatively, you'll make £1 per book sold, but this may be a reduced percentage if the book is discounted (one reason to always read that contract carefully). Unless you're selling tens of thousands of copies, it's probably not going to enable you to quit your day job. You'll find more about royalties and book sales in Chapter six by the way.

Finding your why...

Thinking about why you want to write can be an important part of pitching your work and in motivating yourself. All writers need to have their reason to write. It helps structure your work and hone your language. Who are you writing for? Why? What do you want your book to do? Being clear on this not only leads to a more effective writing and promotional style but can help motivate you through those days where you feel you can't write another word or think about books ever again.

Knowing your 'why' is especially important if you think that you have more than one book in you. Writing one book could just be an act of catharsis to get something off your chest. If you're contemplating a second (or third) there must be something that drives you. Figuring out your main reason for writing can help you make ongoing time for it in your life, create a long-term writing plan and help persuade others close to you (and whose support or understanding you might need) that what you are doing is important.

There are many differences between being a professional versus an amateur writer. Probably the most significant one is that generally speaking, a professional author's primary work or career is in publishing books, whereas an amateur writer does not rely on income solely from writing, or writes alongside other work. Are you an author after writing one book? Perhaps. Or maybe it's about your state of mind – we'll leave you to form your own opinion on this.

Lyndsey finds it extraordinarily satisfying to organise her thoughts into something that benefits thousands of people. That's her why. For Amy it's about being able to craft evidence-based arguments without anyone interrupting - also for the benefit of others. You need to find your why (or whys) and own it. Then on those days when you're staring at your computer screen questioning your life choices you can remind yourself of how important it is to bring new ideas to the masses, share your expertise, challenge established practice, or make yourself known.

If you're still weighing up whether you have the time, resources, skill and emotional energy to write your book, try flipping the question on its head. What would happen if your book wasn't written? Or what *wouldn't* happen if it stayed in your head? Who would miss out, and what would be the consequence of that? How would you feel?

Sometimes, we can redefine our priorities by thinking about the ramifications of *not* doing something. If contemplating not writing your book makes you feel sad, nervous, or fired up - that's probably your cue to keep reading this book and start getting excited about your writing.

How do you know that you are ready to write a book?

If you've bought this book and have got this far (rather than it sitting in your to-be-read pile) you probably have a book idea in mind. So how do you know that it's time to get started? Book excitement is a thing, but before you start...

- Do you have the experience you need?
- Do you have the time?
- Do you have the resources you need?
- Does your book genuinely fill a gap?

Your answers to these questions don't necessarily prevent you from getting started but they might help hone your expectations of how long your writing project may take. There are no medals for writing books quickly and many people develop their first book in particular as a longer labour of love alongside other projects. Likewise, if you're going to write this alongside other life tasks then all you might need is a laptop and an internet connection. And in terms of a gap, well just how important a gap it is (to a broader audience) may determine how wide reaching your book is. But a wide readership as we know is not the only reason to write.

As you ponder whether you have the time to write this book there are a few things to consider. It is not just about the physical time spent writing, but also the emotional time. Writing will take some of your headspace away from your family, partner, friends, work, and hobbies. It is not always a one-off project either. The vast majority of writers do not have the luxury of taking a solid year off to write their manuscript. Books end up being fitted in around the corners of our pre-existing commitments. If there isn't enough time to breathe right now, you may have to put this off until life eases up a little. Writing can be a huge pleasure, but it is also stressful – if life is already throwing curveballs, this additional pressure may be too much.

In all the 'Am I ready' contemplation, you will also need to get practical. Do you have the resources you need – emotional, practical, and any other that you can think of? Do you need to clear a space to work, a new laptop, any research materials? Will you need the support of anyone close to you?

In considering your book's subject matter, we will come back to this point, but have a really deep, honest think about whether your book truly fills a gap in the market. Is this book truly necessary? Do masses of people need it? Is this really a topic about which you should write a whole book, or is it really a blog series, or chapter within a larger book? Super niche topics do not necessarily require an entire 50-90k word manuscript, and trying to force it may be difficult for you to write, justify and market. If you can't honestly say that this book is necessary, it doesn't mean you're not a writer, but think hard about whether this specific book is needed. It's much better to be honest with yourself about this before you spend months writing – after all, you write so that your book will be read. Be sure there is demand before you create the supply. However, saying that, what counts as 'demand' is up to you - just keep those royalty expectations realistic.

The tougher question in that list to reflect on, albeit one many people ask (either out loud or to themselves), is whether you have the experience and credibility to write this book. This is a hard question to ponder without emotion, but try to be objective. It will also depend to some extent on the aim of your book. If you are writing a book about your lived experience then of course you have enough experience by definition to write your book. If however you are giving advice or collating evidence then having sufficient skill and experience is important both in terms of accuracy and credibility.

It is possible that your answer to this question might be 'not yet', which certainly doesn't mean you shouldn't start developing your book idea but might determine how much growing you might need to do before it is ready. Many people spend several years in their field before they write, and this vast experience not only informs your writing, but also will make the writing process easier for you as you will know your subject inside out. It took Amy for example ten years from the start of her PhD to pluck up the courage to write her first book but it then only took her a few months to write it alongside other commitments. Similarly, Lyndsey had spent fifteen years working with families professionally before embarking on writing about it.

We're not saying that you need a solid decade of experience before you start to write, because everyone consolidates learning experiences differently, but it is worth considering. Reflecting on your experience is an important question, because it's a fact of writing life that people will question why *you* are qualified to write your book (as opposed to someone else in the field). Expect this question to come up, and make sure that you've critically appraised it yourself before anyone else does.

Reflecting on your own experience can be challenging as for every person who is overly confident there is at least another, if not more, who unnecessarily doubts their skill or experience. We've both been there and that's why we cover some of these tricky emotions in this book (especially in Chapter eight - Impostor Syndrome). If you're struggling to think about where your experience comes from you might like to think about your experience across the following elements:

- Qualifications and training
- Professional experience
- Research and academic experience
- Voluntary and community work
- Supporting friends and family
- Your own lived experience

There is no hierarchy of experience. All experience is important and can underpin your expertise. However, the type of experience may determine the style of book you write and who your intended audience is. For example, as an academic and researcher Amy leans towards books that bring together research evidence, sometimes presenting detailed studies to construct an argument (with hundreds of references) and sometimes applying that evidence to parent focussed books. She stays away from writing clinically focussed books such as those written by Lyndsey. Conversely to Amy, as a practitioner Lyndsey tends to apply theory to practice, thus supporting parents and professionals to feel equipped and confident. This usually involves a similar number of academic references, but the topics and application are subtly different.

Also, think about whether your professional skill is mostly experiential, or informed by evidence. To write a credible book you'll need to really understand the current thinking and evidence-base. Sometimes, when we work in a niche area, we can get bogged down in the day-to-day practical work without staying abreast of progress or changes in recommendations for practice. Practical, hands-on experience is a wonderful thing, but it becomes something even more magical when it is combined with scientifically backed information.

Finally, it's sensible to ask yourself some hard questions about your writing experience. You may be an expert in your field either professionally, academically or clinically, but this does not automatically make someone a great writer. You may have the knowledge, skills, and even the evidence-base – but can you translate this in a way that others can understand? Again, don't lose hope if you don't have a lot of writing experience but it is good to be aware of which skills you might need to develop and the time that might take.

You may need to spend some time polishing your writing skills and testing them out on different audiences, perhaps through more active blogging. You might need to allow a little more time to draft, redraft, edit and sharpen your manuscript even before you submit it for professional editing. These challenges are so common when you are first starting out as a writer and this is why we've included lots of sections on writing style and improving your writing in this book.

One reason why book writing can feel like a momentous challenge is that it really does test a variety of skills. It brings together your subject expertise, your ability to critique evidence and demands that you hone your writing skills. It feels like a challenge because it is a challenge! One that we would very much argue is worth pursuing, but setting realistic goals helps both structure your book and protect your wellbeing if you find things take longer than you imagined.

Chapter 2

Your writing responsibilities

Writing is a responsibility. There is a difference between simply putting words on paper to create a book, and writing in a way that is thoughtful, effective and evidence based. You'll be putting out information into the world, and people will – quite reasonably – expect that information to be of high quality. But how do you make your work high quality? Your reader expects great things from your book – which is not unreasonable, as they've parted with hard-earned cash to get their hands on it. And more than that, they want to enjoy their time reading your work, or might have high hopes for how it's going to help inform them, or even change their lives. We think there are 6 big responsibilities that you have with your writing that help turn your book from words on a page to a page turner:

1. Accuracy

It should probably go without saying that your writing needs to be accurate. Make sure you have spent a decent amount of time (longer than you probably think it will take) fact-checking, proof reading and trying to spot factual errors. The ideal is that if someone wants to check something, they should be able to easily cross-check this with the original evidence. Try not to use secondary sources (such as contemporary articles, blogs, media stories and books) for information, but go to the original source. Above all, make sure you're not cherry-picking evidence that happens to agree with your view.

We'll come back to how to find and use evidence later on, but for now, suffice it to say that if your work lacks accuracy, someone will jump on it. So check your facts before you submit your work – the nature of publishing is that once it's printed, it's printed. It's not like a blog that you can quickly update or edit (although if you are self-publishing you will have more flexibility). Publishing a second edition can be quite an undertaking, and it certainly isn't something that your publisher is likely to agree to within 3-5 years of the first edition. So if there's a mistake – you (and your readers) will have to live with it.

If you are in doubt about the accuracy of what you are writing then do not be afraid to reach out for support. For example, if it is an academic paper you are reading and are not 100% sure you are understanding the analysis, email the author of the paper to clarify. They would much rather you got it right rather than describe their work inaccurately. If you are unsure about whether you are describing a concept well or in sufficient detail you could reach out to a colleague or someone else in your field. Plenty of authors have their work fact checked (at least in part) by others but if you are doing this to any large extent consider a) paying them (and certainly acknowledging their help in the book) and b) reflecting on whether you have enough knowledge (yet) to be presenting yourself as the expert on this. Do you need to spend more time researching?

2. Ease of reading

Beautifully written phrases shouldn't detract/distract from your message - they should make it easier to understand. Your writing should capture people and make them want to read more. Grammar and punctuation make books, and therefore your message, easier to digest. Your laptop will spell check and also do some basic grammar checking, but it's best not to think of this as anything but a first pass screening.

Some of this work will be done by your editor as well, but you should definitely spend some time checking whether your sentences flow, make sense, and any emphasis with italics and punctuation is correct. Heavy editing is firstly very time consuming, and if you are self-publishing it will also be very expensive! It is also difficult if the editing loses the essence of what you were trying to say. So, put the work in as you write, and check your phrases and paragraphs often – your editor, and your reader will thank you.

On this note, it can be worth reading your work out loud to yourself. Is the punctuation and emphasis in the correct place? Does it flow or do you have overly long sentences that someone trying to read out loud would struggle with? This can be important if you decide to audio record your book at any stage. It's not just about getting the facts down on paper but crafting them so that you speak to the reader.

Finally, don't feel that you have to be academic or verbose in your language. Simple writing and phrases can be very effective and appeal to a wider audience. It could be that some sentences need careful crafting and mastery but if you find yourself taking hours to write a paragraph it might be time to pause and ask yourself whether you are overcomplicating this (or procrastinating for some reason). Fancy language does not indicate expert knowledge and vice versa.

3. Credibility

Your experience, knowledge, or skills are what make you the most appropriate person to write your book. This refers not only to the credibility you have within your field, but also your skill of conveying this to your readers. In an era where anyone can publish an ebook quickly and cheaply, you will need to demonstrate your credibility. Having critically considered whether you have the required experience, skill and resources to write your book, you then need to reassure your reader of your expertise. This helps them to pick your book up in the first place, trust you, and continue reading. Be confident and bold. If you have good information to share, then make sure you tell your reader why they should listen to you.

There's another important point about credibility though that is worth mentioning. Experience and qualifications are entirely different, and we need to honestly consider ours in order to stay safe and within the role that we are portraying as a writer. We discussed this briefly in the context of whether you have enough experience to write your book, but you also need to separate experiencing a particular scenario or event, and being someone who is qualified to teach about or treat that condition or circumstance.

There are dozens of examples of where we need to be careful to stay within our scope of practice. For example, as parents we have years of experience of being immersed in the world of education and teaching, but this does not qualify us to speak about the evidence and theories of teaching children. As a paediatric nurse, Lyndsey is not qualified to speak authoritatively about adult healthcare, mental health nursing, or even a subspecialty of paediatrics, like neonatal intensive care. Amy is often asked to comment on nutrient profiles or allergy development and politely declines as this is a huge leap from her expertise in psychology and public health. Knowing when to accept the difference between experience and qualification and the requirement to signpost to someone better qualified is an important skill.

We must be careful that we have the qualifications and experience to write about what we're writing, or that we make it clear that we are writing from a lay person's perspective (which is valid, as long as people understand that this is what you are doing). It is absolutely ok to reflect on situations when you have been in receipt of another person's expertise. But allowing people to assume that you have expertise because you are writing about an area when you do not is unethical. Not everyone buying your book will have the critical thinking skills to know how to check whether you are qualified to write it meaning that yes you may well still sell books about something you have no real knowledge in writing, but is that really fair?

So what is the difference between all these attributes? Do you need all of these? Are there exceptions? We feel that there are distinct differences between these attributes:

Fascination: We are naturally drawn to topics that interest us, either because we have had some personal experience, or just find something really intriguing. Passion and fascination help bring our writing to life - there's nothing worse than thinking your writer is bored by the topic. However, we must be really careful to distinguish between writing about something that we find really interesting, and having the knowledge, credentials or training to back up this fascination.

We may well be fascinated by a topic and really want to know more but that doesn't mean we can write about it as experts simply because we find it interesting. Interest is not necessarily synonymous with expertise, until it is backed up by appropriate levels of experience and knowledge. That's not to say we can't write about what fascinates us, we just need to be clear that we're in the 'fascinated camp' i.e. *intrigued, curious,* or *captivated* by a topic or question that we think is really important, rather than presenting ourselves as the informed experts.

Knowledge: Rather as the word implies, knowledge is about what you know - although there are different depths to knowledge. Albert Einstein once said *"Any fool can know. The point is to understand."* This sounds a little harsh, but it really is about applying knowledge. Knowledge is a wonderful thing but, in and of itself, it is not enough. We might know about sourdough, and maybe have baked our own loaf a few times, but that doesn't mean we have enough skill, experience or ability to translate that knowledge into the definitive sourdough recipe book.

Knowledge can perhaps be gained from reading a book, or a paper, but it's what you do with that knowledge that is the critical next step. Theoretical knowledge is different from applying the knowledge in practice, testing it, refining and developing it. This transition is what enables a practitioner to progress from someone who understands the theory, to being able to apply and adapt the theory to a variety of situations and nuances. Is there some training or experience you need to gain in order to write authoritatively about your topic?

Experience: This may take several forms. It could be interpreted as having considerable experience in a particular profession, or working with a group of people. It may relate to life experience. We don't necessarily need a peer-reviewed paper to our name if what we are referring to is our personal lived experience. Frankly, many areas are under-researched, and it would be inappropriate to disregard something because there is no research. However, if it is a topic about which there is plenty of literature, it is best to at least refer to it - even if you then point out the gaps or holes. Experience is valuable, and sometimes it is worth more if the experience is unusual, or about an under-studied subject or community. Just be clear about when you speak from experience, and what this experience is. Experience that is paired with knowledge is a powerful combination.

Training: Training courses, online learning, and taught programmes are great. Continued professional development is part of our lifelong learning. They are not the same as putting the training into practice though, or that the training is up to date. Some people have CVs that are peppered with training courses - but that doesn't mean they are competent. Once upon a time Lyndsey was a highly competent paediatric nurse with dozens of clinical skills courses under her belt, but for many years has been non-clinical. She would be the first to say that you probably want someone with more up to date experience caring for your critically sick child than her. Training - however wonderful, does not equal current expertise.

Credentials: Training and credentials sometimes go hand in hand, but not always. Not all courses or training provide a credential. They are normally gained after a substantial period of study and following some kind of assessment of skills and knowledge. It is certainly a way to benchmark particular competencies and ensure a minimum level of safety, skill and knowledge. But a newly credentialed person does not have the same experience as someone with more years of working in that field. Also, try not to be tempted to use your credentials gained in one area to give legitimacy when writing about a topic you know very little about. One to watch out for when considering whether someone has the expertise in a topic they are writing about is the misuse of a title such as 'Dr'. They may well indeed have a PhD. But if the PhD is in astrophysics is it being used fairly if they are writing about childcare?

Lived experience: There will be times when your lived experience is far more valuable than any credential. Perhaps you are from an under-represented group - your experience is incredibly useful, and maybe the existing literature is irrelevant or inappropriate. Maybe you've been through a traumatic event and you are speaking of that experience. On other occasions it would be entirely inappropriate to cite your personal experience instead of an established evidence base that was most likely developed by teams of very highly qualified scientific experts and professionals. This is especially important when you are talking about something that has a safety aspect, and about which there are established best practice guidelines. If you contradict these guidelines, you won't have a leg to stand on.

Many people will assume credibility and authority from someone who is writing a book, so make absolutely sure you are qualified to write what you're writing. If you are not appropriately qualified, it will be very likely that you may not be aware of recent relevant, topical, subject appropriate research and guidelines, and may miss something vital. This is not only going to do a disservice to those reading the book, but also those who *are* qualified to provide that advice or information. It doesn't mean you can't write a book, but think about whether you need to collaborate, or change the focus of your book slightly.

But equally, if you happen to have the qualifications and expertise needed, then take this as an encouragement to get on and write your book. If you're sick of people who are not qualified, experienced, knowledgeable or skilled enough to be writing books about a subject in which you have those attributes, then there is definitely a market for a book written by someone who knows what they're talking about.

Finally, if the doubts are setting in, do be aware that impostor syndrome and perfectionism make perfectly capable people doubt themselves. If your brain is telling you 'you can't do this, who do you think you are?' - go and check out Chapter eight on dealing with these psychological barriers first.

4. Humility

We know we've just explained the importance of justifying your credibility confidently. However, there's a fine line between knowing that you have important information to share with the skills to deliver that information, and arrogance. Arrogant writing often takes the stance of assuming one way of thinking, ignoring others' expertise and not taking the time to work on further developing your understanding. It's off-putting and can be dangerous if it spreads poor information.

However, it's important that even as experienced authors, we remain teachable and aware of our place on the learning curve. You have probably heard of the 'Dunning-Kruger Effect' where people who know the least often, ironically, overestimate just how much they know. As you develop as a writer you'll probably start to experience the opposite of this - the horror at just how much information that is out there to pick through and understand.

This process can feel overwhelming but is important both in developing your work and keeping that humility. Most people start off knowing they have a lot to learn but as they attend some training, or do some reading they ascend up what many people colloquially refer to as 'Mount Stupid'. This is basically where a little bit of knowledge can lead some people to believe they know more than they really do. As we acquire more learning post Mount Stupid we begin to realise the enormity of the subject, entering what is known as the 'Valley of Despair'. More learning begins to reduce this despair, but to cut a long story short - the more you know, the more you realise there is a lot left to learn. This perspective is important.

We also need to acknowledge the role that others have had in our learning. You should do this throughout your writing by citing those that have produced the research that you are now relying on to make your point. Even if the research is your own, it is likely that you stood on the shoulders of others to produce it. You may also want to acknowledge people in your introduction, dedication or acknowledgements. There is more on the importance of this in Chapters 10 and 11 - Understanding Evidence and Referencing.

Humility also means the confidence to admit when you are wrong or your views take a new direction. You will occasionally write something and then come across more research that changes your take on a topic. You might attend training that helps makes better sense of something, and you'll wish you had known that before your book was published. This is just life. Having an attitude of humility helps you to handle this, and also to write in such a way as to make it obvious to your reader that research is constantly being refined – therefore they should expect that recommendations may alter slightly. Never be afraid to say that in the light of new evidence and understanding you've changed your mind, or your viewpoint has shifted.

Humility also means acknowledging that not everyone finds your topic as fascinating as you do (ouch!). This is why you need to make your writing easy and enjoyable to read. A certain statistics textbook was written by an author who does not take himself, or his subject too seriously and we deeply appreciate the tone of his writing. Frankly, there is nothing that can make a statistical software package more riveting for most people, but at least the author demonstrates self-awareness of the turgidity of his subject through self-deprecating comments, anecdotes and satire. This is a tricky balance to get right - because obviously you would buy a book like this to help you grapple with stats. If you just wanted a giggle, you'd have bought a joke book. However, if you can walk this fine line it will elevate the quality of your writing and keep your reader engaged.

Finally, taking a humble approach to your writing means that you do not make assumptions about what your reader already knows. Consider as you write, the possibility that they know more than you do. We know – a daunting thought! But all is not lost if you write with that awareness. Sometimes people appreciate having an affirmation of what they already know. They also may have a lot of knowledge but struggle with writing skills or finding the time to write a book (or have no intention of ever doing such a crazy thing!).

Equally, think about those for whom your subject is uncharted territory. You may wonder how on earth you write for both experts and novices alike. Well, you provide a learning journey – taking them from the basic to the more advanced, but explaining it clearly and simply as you go. You acknowledge that some of the information may be too much, or too basic – acting as revision.

We have both previously written about fairly dry subjects because they are needed for completing the coverage of a topic. But rather than expecting everyone to read the entire chapter, we preface the nerdiest parts with 'permission' to skip a certain section, with the reassurance that taking the short-cut will not affect the flow of the rest of the chapter. Giving your reader little breaks like this can sometimes be really helpful but it does require some self-awareness and thoughtfulness, as well as a bit of planning of the chapter content to enable readers to skip parts without losing the meaning of the entire section.

5. Honesty

While you may be well qualified to write your book, you need to be honest with your reader about its limitations. There will inevitably be gaps in research, areas that have patchy information, and where you are using experience to get you through the guesswork. This is fine if you're honest about it. We would also suggest you are honest about yourself as a writer. Acknowledge your privilege, experience, learning gaps, and biases. Literally everyone has something to disclose. This is fine, as long as you are open about it. For example, Amy chose to openly reflect on her own personal experiences and biases in the introduction to her book 'Informed is best', both as good practice in a book that tackled the issue of bias in research but also because being transparent is an important part of readers trusting you and knowing that you are aware that no writer is completely unbiased.

We are all influenced by our contexts, circumstances, experiences, biases, and our mood. If you know you are writing with a chip on your shoulder or a point to prove, write it down by all means, but then come back to what you've written when you feel calmer and sense check it. Writing something down is often cathartic so it can be helpful sometimes to get it off your chest, and then edit it (or delete it) later after you have processed your feelings about it. It's not a waste of time – after all, writing is not just for your reader's benefit, but for yours. Just ensure that you're not inadvertently having a public rant. Some writing should be kept for an audience of one.

At the start of every conference presentation, the speaker is usually required to acknowledge their conflicts of interest, biases or disclosures. Many people also take the opportunity to be reflective of their privilege, opportunities and those they are indebted to. In many ways a book needs a written version of this to provide the reader with some context. You often find this in an introduction. Give your reader a bit of background about you as a professional, and as a human.

6. Good communication

A good title and a solid blurb will make people pick up your book. Rave reviews might persuade them to buy it. But well written text is what will make them read it. Well-written books are like a killer recipe that's been passed down your family. They need just the right amounts of ingredients to make them work. Like a cake with too little egg, a book lacking the right ingredients for your reader will fall flat. You might find this frustrating if you know what you're talking about and just want to get to the point, but unless your reader is as passionate about your subject as you are, they'll need more to keep them hooked.

Using tools and techniques to help your reader

There are many ways you can make it easier for your reader to stay with you. You don't have to use all of these – some of them might make you cringe if they're not your style. That's ok – think of them like tools. Nobody needs the entire contents of their toolbox for putting up a picture on the wall. But they might need a different tool if they are tackling the horror of flat pack furniture. In the same way, we can use different literary 'tools' for different forms of writing. Here are some tools that you can keep in your writing 'toolkit' to help shape your work:

Analogies can be a really good way of bringing clarity and explanation to something that you're trying to convey to your reader by helping them think about something unrelated but similar.

Humour is another tool (in the right balance) that you could consider. Now, if this feels wholly unnatural you can ignore this one. Unless you naturally use self-deprecating humour, sarcasm, satire or irony, these particular tools can sound forced if you're not careful. But in general, wit and humour make text easier on the brain and provide welcome relief from serious content.

Vignettes are a good way to relate theory to practice. You can try presenting a short case study, story or outline to help your reader see the relevance of something to their practice. Lyndsey often uses them when trying to make a case for practice change that might feel accusatory if it is perceived to come from one professional to another. However, the same message in a vignette explaining in a parent or patient's words makes the impact often easier to accept.

Quotes can be incredibly powerful when you're trying to make an argument for something. Amy uses quotes from her research to tell a story in someone's own words. Other people use quotes from well-known speakers, public figures or authors. They can be very punchy and impactful when used well. You definitely don't want to overdo this though, as they lose their power in large quantities.

Having a clear voice is one of your authoring tasks. Your writing should allow your personality to come through. Our editor refers to this as 'writing as you speak'. This style of writing feels 'warm' to a reader and makes them feel that they might be having a conversation (albeit a rather one-sided one!) with someone they know and respect.

There are some other ways you can help your reader to not lose the proverbial plot:

- Make sure that the language you're using is appropriate for your ideal reader. If you're writing an entry level nonfiction text, or a book on a relatively unknown subject about which many people will be unfamiliar, you'll want to avoid the use of too much jargon. It's exhausting to have to keep referring back to a glossary, so be considerate to your reader and explain terms simply if you can. However sometimes using long words is unavoidable.
- Break text up so large chunks of writing don't feel like an assault on the eye. Bullet points or numbered lists work well, as can diagrams, tables and photos. You could use quotes or highlight boxes to pick out something you'd like to draw your reader's attention to.

- Be careful with punctuation. When Lyndsey was in high school an English teacher used to ban the 'comma sprinkler'. She was referring to death by comma - the tendency to scatter commas all over the page. Commas are wonderful but be careful that they're inserted in the right place, or you can lose the entire meaning of the sentence.
- Consider sentence length. To some extent this depends on the type of book you're writing. In general, the longer the sentence the harder the text is to read. A long sentence isn't 'wrong', but you need to be careful that *all* your text isn't like that. Conventional wisdom is that a sentence of 15-20 words is about right.
- You can break your text up with paragraphs and subheadings. Paragraphs are usually used to introduce new ideas. However, if you are explaining something very complex it is still appropriate to start new paragraphs when you make a subsequent point, even if you haven't shifted to a new concept or idea yet. Continuous text that runs over a page feels daunting. Subheadings can be used to change the subject. If you were reading out loud, think of paragraphs as a short pause in a speech, and subheadings as a longer pause with a sip of water for good measure.

Finally, we do need to talk about the skill of writing. Don't worry, we're not going to lecture you on passive voice, the taboo of the split infinitive, or the controversial use of a verb (that's up to your editor!). However, it should probably go without saying that your writing needs to flow, the chapters need to follow a logical order, and the sentences need to be well-constructed. This is not a job that can just be left to a really gifted editor because the tone and meaning of your writing will be lost with heavy editing.

When you write you are essentially a literary servant. Your writing needs to be easy and enjoyable to read or you will lose people on the way. Communication can take many forms, and not all of them are appropriate in every context. Learning to adapt your writing to your audience is a skill that is definitely worth it in the long run.

Chapter 3

Your book topic and audience

Before Lyndsey wrote her first book she had a concept in mind for a completely different book. It was a subject in which she was competent and equipped to write, and she was excited to get started. She thought of a title, planned out the chapters, visualised the cover, and fantasised about the major publishing house that was certainly going to bite her hand off to get this book. You can probably guess what happened – when she started to do the task we are about to recommend to you she found that her book had already been written, by someone significantly more famous we might add. She was crushed at the time but now laughs about it because, as we will tell you, there is always room for another book.

However, we caveat that statement slightly by cautioning that you certainly need to do your research. It's fine to write a book about a subject that is well supplied with literary material, but the more competition there is, the harder it's going to be to persuade a publisher to take your book. A good place to start is by thinking of all the words people might type into Amazon (or any online bookshop) to find a book on the subject they want information on. Start with searching for a book with your title - if you've already thought of one. This is always helpful, because a similar book with the same title almost certainly won't fly without a bit of a re-think. Then switch out the words to see what other books about similar topics are already available. You might be surprised how many books are out there that you knew nothing about – even if this is your special subject. Of course they're not all going to be Sunday Times bestseller books, but it's wise to know how crowded the space is.

After you've gone through this process one of several things may happen. You might find that your book is really niche. This could be a good thing in that it won't have any significant competition. However, you need to honestly ask yourself if it is *so* niche there isn't really a market for it (and how much that matters to you). The second scenario is that you notice that there are a few books already, but either they are really dated, or obscure, and you are pretty convinced that you can do a better job. This is essentially good news.

The third scenario is that, like Lyndsey, you discover that someone really famous, competent and impressive has written your book already. We're not going to lie – this is a blow because it's going to be much harder (though not impossible) to persuade the general public to buy your book over the existing one. You also run the risk, unless your book is significantly different, of being accused of plagiarism or idea stealing which is never fun. The fourth scenario is that you find out that there are several books about your topic, written by many different people – in other words, it's a crowded market albeit one that may still have room for your work.

With either scenario 3 or 4 you do have some options, so don't despair. One option is to slightly change the angle, style, or focus. You could also take the topic in a new and different direction, breathing fresh life into something that feels 'done to death'. Another option is to look at a similar topic and make your book more expansive than you originally planned. If you feel confident that your style and take on this subject is significantly different then you may decide to go ahead anyway. Both of us have written books on topics that are in fairly crowded markets – a bit of healthy competition can be a good thing.

One advantage of writing in a crowded market is that you do not need to feel that you should write a 'vanilla' book that covers everything. You can really make your author's voice come alive and write for a very specific audience – knowing that your reader has consciously chosen your book for its perspective amidst a sea of books offering something slightly different.

Finally, you may need to think truthfully about how marketable your book is. It can help to canvas some opinions from others who are less immersed in the topic than you. If we're really honest with ourselves, we can sometimes get excited about a topic and truly believe that everyone on earth needs to know about it – such as ... the mating behaviours of horseflies! If this happens to be your specialist topic then no doubt you are extremely learned in the fascinating world of horseflies.

However, we hate to break it to you but it could well be that most people are happy to let their life go by with no information on your subject. Niche is good. Uber-niche is risky. Aside from your friends and family (who may be biased, let's face it), what other evidence do you have that your book would sell well? How does the topic come up in your world? Do people ask you constantly? Is it a frequently Googled question? Try looking on https://answerthepublic.com/ to see if it is. Do you observe confusion in this subject that your book would address? You'll need to be able to justify why your book needs to be written.

Where will your book sit on the shelves?

Once you've worked out who your literary competition is and whether there is a market for your book, you will need to figure out the answer to another important question. Something that almost every literary agent and publisher will want to know is where your book fits into the book world. In fact, they may even ask this when you write your book proposal and chapter outline.

Within the broad categories of fiction and nonfiction, books are sub-categorized to help readers find what they want. Essentially, if you walked into a large bookshop, in which section would your book be located? Will it be under 'history', 'parenting', 'autobiography', 'natural world', 'health', 'gardening', 'crime' or whatever? Where does your book fit in? Or where would you like it to?

This is closely related to the issue of competition and similar books. How well do the books on the same shelf as yours sell? You can check their sales rankings on Amazon to give you an idea. Amazon produces a ranking of *all* the books it lists for sale, with one being the best-selling. It changes regularly based on how many copies a book is selling. It also ranks books by category so although you would need fantastic books sales to be within the top ten of all books, you may have a stronger chance of being within the top ten selling books in your category.

Look at the competition in your likely category (i.e. parenting, self-help, nutrition) to get a feel for which books are popular and which ones lurk down at rank 1.3M (which is nobody's favourite place to be). What do you need to do to be different and stand out?

Another worthwhile activity is to research how much those other books sell for. If the average RRP is £9.99 you may struggle to sell yours for £19.99, even if there was a justifiable reason for this price differential. Your book may be better, but sometimes a potential book reader will simply choose a more affordable book, unless you can persuade them very quickly otherwise. Remember, they are unlikely to read *both* books and then compare and contrast. They will most likely pick one over the other. It's harsh, but true.

What will your writing style look like?

Perhaps you already have a writing style, and have a good idea how your book is going to sound. Or maybe you've not written more than a blog post since you were in school, or university. It's a good idea to spend some time thinking about the tone and style of your writing. By this we mean, will it be chatty? Heavily referenced? Humorous? Empathic? Challenging? None of these styles are better or more appropriate per se, but the tone and style of your book may affect how it is received. This is partly about making the book enjoyable for your reader, enabling you to convey your message effectively, and also so that you are recognizable through your writing.

If you've not given much thought to your writing style, perhaps think instead about who inspires you? Which writers keep you hooked? You can have a bit of fun with this because there are almost infinite styles of writing. One of the best ways to improve your writing is by reading lots of books to work out what style of writing appeals. Read lots of different styles of books, published by people from different cultures and time periods. By doing this you will subconsciously gain inspiration from other writers, and hone your personal style.

If you prefer reading fiction and are put off by reading numerous nonfiction books to expand your style, then just read what you enjoy. Reading fiction can be really helpful to your writing. Don't think that reading Celeste Ng is irrelevant if you're writing a reference book. Reading Austen might add poetry and beautiful adjectives to your nonfiction (though avoid if you're trying to combat wordiness!). Reading Tolkien might add rich description to your memoir. All reading is valuable when it comes to learning more about your style, what you like, and expanding your vocabulary.

This is also a good strategy to work out what you *dis*like. What writing styles bore you? Have you ever read a book and vowed to never read another by the same author? If so, what didn't you like about it? You don't have to overthink how you will adjust your writing. Simply by exposing yourself to a lot of different literary styles, you will absorb ideas of how to improve your phrasing and the cadence of your sentences.

Developing your inspiration

We are often inspired by an eclectic mix of life experiences, authors, thought leaders, speakers and events. All this may influence your writing, or bring concepts together in new and creative ways. When you're thinking about writing, you can use ideas from disparate subjects to influence the topic you want to write about. Perhaps you can see how drawing on a theory from one discipline could be applied in a completely new way to your subject. This brings a freshness and originality to your work and will make people think.

Perhaps there is a book you admire, but it's dated and research has moved on. Or maybe there's a popular book on a separate but related topic – you can look at what seems to work well in that book and let that influence yours. It's important to note that we do not mean re-wording someone else's work, if you're not sure check out the section on plagiarism later on in this book. Your work should be genuinely unique and take an idea forward.

It's very likely that you have a different take on an existing topic. If you have enough expertise and credibility to write a book about your topic, and there happen to be plenty of other books – don't be put off. We've already said that we have written books about topics that have a crowded market, but the reason there is room for more is that a new perspective provides your reader with an alternative approach.

You may also have new information to add, or be able to update and improve on existing work. Perhaps there's a book that is written for one level of reading ability or cognitive understanding – you could write a book that is simpler to understand, or conversely adds evidence and further explanation.

For example, Lyndsey wrote her first sleep book for health and childcare professionals because there were hundreds of easy-to-read books aimed at parents which had very little evidence base, and there were also several books written for sleep doctors which were very nerdy and niche. Her book filled a gap. Later she also wrote a book for parents. Risky, you might think, given the highly crowded sleep book market; but again it filled a gap because there weren't many books that were written ostensibly for parents and full of evidence-based information.

Don't be put off by the number of books. No book works for every situation or type of reader, so as long as yours genuinely fills a gap there's a place for it. Recycling ideas or topics is arguably essential in the literary world because evidence is always being updated and improved, thus rendering older books out of date and ushering in your book as the latest resource on a given topic.

Being unique

It can be daunting to face the competition for your book and write it anyway. To visualise those packed shelves and wonder how to make yours stand out and offer something unique and special. This thought process can be overwhelming and is a fast track to inertia. Don't worry about how to make your book better than everyone else's, instead just do what you're good at. The rest will follow automatically.

You write a book that stands out by being yourself. You will inherently bring something unique to your topic through doing this, even if there are 20 books on the same subject. This attitude requires some serious confidence in yourself though, which can feel particularly hard for first-time authors.

People instinctively want to please as many others as possible, not offend, and avoid the dreaded 1* review. So we'll let you into a secret right now. Not everyone will love your book. Some people will hate it. Some people you respect might hate it too (yikes!). It is much better to write a book that feels authentic to you and have people not like it, than to try to write a book that jars with, or waters down your own view and find that, even then, someone doesn't like it. For more on dealing with this see Chapter 17 which is all about criticism.

Trying to appeal to everyone often backfires. Books that do this often end up losing focus, or being a bit bland. Essentially, if you try to write a book to appeal to everyone, you'll end up pleasing no one. Finding your niche is really important. With so much competition, what you don't want to do is go mainstream. Rather than write a vanilla book that you hope will have enough of what everyone needs, be brave and write a chocolate and coconut book. People who hate coconut will hate your book and that's ok, because you will have legions of people who have been waiting forever for someone to create such a unique and brilliant flavour. Similarly, if you write a vegan, gluten-free salted caramel flavour book, all the vegans or people with coeliac disease who have been patiently waiting for the world to catch up and make an ice cream that they can eat will suddenly become your superfans.

The chances are, your book topic is one where people might have different opinions. The idea behind writing very specifically for those who agree with you is that they will feel aligned with what you're saying. When we read a book that tries to have mass appeal, it can feel like the message is diluted. You can actually feel the author trying not to offend, or playing it safe. When we read books like that we end up feeling lukewarm about them. The argument does not always feel compelling.

The other advantage of writing like this is that you are actually less likely to attract the people who will disagree with you in the first place. The kind of people who hold strong views about a topic do not necessarily want to read a book where it feels like the author can't make their mind up about where they stand.

Finally, you will need to believe in your work. Be bold in your writing, avoiding too much apologetics. Readers can often easily spot when an author has been sitting on the fence so long they have splinters. Write with confidence and your reader will be nodding along to every word you write. People who read books that they relate to on a personal and fundamental level are the ones who write glowing reviews and tell all their friends or colleagues.

Who is your audience?

When you begin to plan your book one of the things you will need to consider is who your audience is. We have already said that your personal views on a subject can inform your approach to writing your book, but that doesn't necessarily need to be as restrictive as it sounds. For example, your book may be very specific in its perspective on a topic but it may appeal to a wide variety of people – both students and experts. It may appeal to both lay people and professionals, novices and advanced learners.

On the other hand, you may want to write a book for people who specifically speak your language. The more niche and specific you make it, the more you will probably capture the interest of your intended audience, but you also narrow the market. It's a difficult balance to get right, but don't panic – this is where marketing comes in. If you want to skip ahead, there's more on this in Chapter 13 which discusses skills for promoting your book.

You might also be writing to change hearts and minds. For example, your intended audience might be one with an alternate view to you and whom you specifically try to win around. This is a more challenging task because it requires you to write with conviction, but also tact and diplomacy. We certainly wouldn't want to put you off trying by the way – but you may need a thick skin and a watertight argument.

Considering your readers

Whoever your future readers are, it helps to bear in mind what your typical reader may be like. Consider several questions:

- What is their reading level?
- What do they already know about this subject?
- Why did they buy this book in the first place?
- What do they want you to answer or clear up for them?

Knowing your audience and what they want from you will help you to write a sharp, focused book that meets the needs of your reader. Whether you are writing for impact, to inspire, provoke contemplation, educate, challenge, equip, argue a case, present your research, or provide an alternative narrative, you will need to deliver that clearly to your audience. So think carefully about who they are.

What does your audience expect?

You will also need to think about what your audience expects from your book. In a sense you can do whatever you like as long as it is clear from your title, blurb and marketing. But on the other hand if it is a novel topic, or you are renowned for your expertise in this particular area, then your reader might have certain expectations - such as learning about your research, reading about a new theory, or having some practical recommendations that will help them with a problem they are facing.

If you have a look at reviews a common criticism of many books is that a book is pitched at a certain target audience, for example parents, and is too theoretical and not practical enough. Or it is pitched as an evidence-based text yet skates over the research, or does not back up an argument with enough theory. You can help your reader to know what to expect with a title that tells them exactly what to expect. This, and your back cover blurb is all your reader has to go on before they get into the book. Believe it or not, putting people off buying the wrong book is not necessarily a bad thing.

Have a think about the words you use in your title, and your subtitle if you're going to use one. Some authors use a catchy title that is obscure, witty or clever, but clear up any potential confusion by adding a subtitle. Your blurb can also quickly outline what your reader can expect to learn or consider from reading your book. This is important because you are trying to help potential readers decide between other books and yours.

People buy books for different reasons and they get frustrated when they buy a book that doesn't give them what they want. Let's say a student wants a book about counselling theories but they end up with your self-help book. The self-help book might be wonderful, but having a do-it-yourself guide to cognitive behaviour therapy won't help them write their assignment on the theories of psychotherapy techniques. It's an obvious example, but the point is that you want your reader to love your book, tell everyone how wonderful it is on social media, and keep it. What you don't want is for them to return it to Amazon, leave a 1* review and tell everyone how good a *different* book is. That goes back to our earlier point that putting off *some* readers is not necessarily a bad thing. There's winning people over to your point of view, and there's fighting a losing battle.

Predicting (and using) the criticism

We would all like to bury the idea that some people won't like the book that's just taken us hundreds of hours to think about, plan and write. But life isn't all sunshine and rainbows and the best way to deal with criticism is to expect it, and plan for it - you might want to read more about this in Chapter 17: How to handle criticism.

This is partly where early reviews come in. How many people have you spoken to about your book? Have you taken their suggestions or feedback on board? Have you asked people who will tell you honestly which parts didn't make sense, were waffly, or repetitive? You'll need people who you can trust to be constructive and frank. Doting parents and superfans aren't the best people as they are highly forgiving and will be looking to excuse the less-than-perfect areas. As hard as it is at any point to hear criticism, it's far better to hear it before the book is actually on the shelves and it's too late to fix a problem.

If you have written about a controversial topic you will also probably know what the likely objections to your book will be. Imagine your biggest critic and make a list of all the criticisms or questions you can imagine them throwing at you. Then try to come up with a logical and compelling comeback. Imagine having to squeeze this comeback into the 280 characters of a tweet to really get it succinct. You'll feel a lot more prepared for the criticism when it comes if you do this.

Knowing your audience's pain points

Books tend to do really well when they address a definite need. People often buy non-fiction books to help with a problem - whether that is writing a CV, being more assertive in the workplace, asking someone out on a date, improving their relationship, or learning how to introduce solids to their baby. Books bought for these sorts of purposes do well if they excel at helping people solve these problems. In short, if it's a problem-solving book, make sure you have plenty of practical problem-solving points.

As you plan your book, imagine what your reader will gain from reading it, and also how they will feel if this is not what you deliver. Problem solving books do well with clear topic-driven chapter titles, lots of subheadings which help people navigate to the right place, and other tools such as key points boxes, table, diagrams, graphs and summary sentences or paragraphs.

If you're writing a problem-solver, your most important objective is obviously to help your reader overcome the problem. But that doesn't mean they can't enjoy the book while they learn strategies in the process. You may also want to empathise with them about how they might be feeling about their problem. This will help your reader connect with you and feel like you are writing for them.

For example, if you're writing a book about how to house train your puppy you obviously need to provide enough information about how to achieve this, but you could also include some information about how frustrating it is when your puppy pees on your favourite rug. You could incorporate humour, perhaps by including an amusing anecdote about how your pup once pooped on Great Aunt Agatha's best coat. This is where the balance is important. If there is lots of sympathy about how annoying it is to have to carpet shampoo your entire house, or how expensive it gets to have to keep buying new slippers because they've all been chewed, and several funny stories involving failed toilet training, but no actual practical help - then you're in trouble.

Other books do well because they successfully introduce a concept, or are thought provoking. You may want to help someone understand a problem, rather than solve it. If this sounds like your book then your aim should be to gently challenge, invite contemplation, or inspire debate.

As you read this, you might want to consider the type of reader who will buy your book. Be as specific as you can, because this will help you write the book they need. Will your reader be a well-informed academic who will expect and demand evidence along with theoretical underpinning? Or will they be an exhausted and overwhelmed parent who needs the summary at the end of the too-long-didn't-read (TLDR) chapter? Will they be a professional looking for a new approach to solve a problem, or are they a curiously minded lazy-Sunday afternoon reader?

Do you want your book to change hearts and minds? Do you want to improve practice? Are you trying to offer a new approach? The more specific you can be, and the better you meet the likely needs of your intended audience, the more they will love it. Understanding your target audience will also help your publisher (if you have one) to pitch your book to the right people, in the right way.

Different types of writing/different audiences

It is also very likely that writing books isn't the only type of writing you do. Often writing a book is a gateway to other written work, even if this is just to promote your work. Many authors find that not only do they have another book in them but they also need to write articles, features, blogs, social media posts and other written material.

Sometimes these pieces of written work will be about the same subject as your book, and it can feel overwhelming to try to summarise your 90k word book into a 500-word article or blog. But remember, these two types of writing have entirely different purposes, and indeed, the people who read your article or blog might not even buy your book.

To keep this simple, when you're trying to write about a massive topic succinctly, you have two main options - zooming in, or zooming out:

Zoom in

When you zoom in, you accept that you cannot possibly cover all the information that you know and understand in a small piece of writing and still do it justice. So you decide to focus on one very specific and niche part of the puzzle. By doing this you can do justice to the level of detail you would usually provide on your topic. You are also able to demonstrate the extent and depth of your knowledge. This approach leaves your reader wanting more, and also believing that you will have this level of knowledge about other related aspects of this topic as well.

Zooming in provides a valuable piece of information, but does not give away the entire plot. This particular tactic also means that you have probably got an infinite number of topics to explore with subsequent pieces of writing, which is useful if you know you will have to keep producing written content. It's also a really good way for you to broaden your understanding of your subject, as it will force you to drill down into a very narrow topic. In fact, this approach can often be a good way to gain inspiration for future books.... You have been warned!

Zoom out

By contrast then, zooming out is when you look at the macro-topic. In many ways this may remind you of your book proposal (see Chapter five). If you decide to zoom out you want to give your reader the TLDR overview of your book. Zooming out can be a really good way of explaining how vast a topic is whilst helping people to understand what they don't know (and why they need to buy your book to fill in the gaps!).

This potentially is a strategy that has less longevity than zooming in; although in practice many people of course combine different approaches depending on the feature they are writing. There are, however, ways that you can zoom out multiple times, in unique ways. You could, for instance, look at the macro-structure from different perspectives or priorities. For example, you could summarise some of your understanding of infant feeding from the perspectives of the infant, parents, grandparents, siblings, policy makers or midwives. It will be similar information at the heart, but the priorities, tone and content will be subtly different, and adds layers of complexity and fresh thinking.

Chapter 4

Who will publish your book? And what if they don't?

So you have an idea for your book, maybe even a drafted manuscript – where do you go from here? It could be that you are in the relatively rare position that a publisher approached you asking if you would like to write a book. But for most people, at least for their first book, it's likely that you will be the one deciding where you would ideally like to pitch your book to be published.

It's a good idea to think about where you will publish your book from the outset. The type of publisher may determine things such as whether you need to write a book proposal (and in what form), the style and length of your book, and maybe even your time scale. Although you may wish (or need) to pitch to multiple publishers, checking out their guidelines for submissions and looking at work they have already published can help guide any proposal or book structure that you create.

In terms of who will publish your book you have two broad main options. You can either self-publish or you can pitch the idea to a book publisher who will publish it for you.

Pros and cons of self-publishing

Self-publishing has become an increasingly popular option for many writers who wish to retain more control of their work in recent years. This ease of publication and flexibility has led to some great works being published, alongside shall we say some more dubious pieces. Although the lack of hoops to jump through enables brilliant writers to bypass hurdles (and biases), it also allows just about anyone to publish and that can, often unfairly, affect the reputation of self-published work.

Whether you choose to take this route is something that only you can decide. There are many advantages and disadvantages to self-publishing and your decision may vary across books depending on your aims and motivation for writing them.

Some benefits of self-publishing:

- It may be quicker to publish your book and see it available to purchase.
- You will make more money per book sold.
- It gives you access to some of the biggest book sales platforms of today (such as Amazon).
- You have more freedom in terms of what you write, how you write, the style of your book, even down to minor details like the title of your book.
- You have more flexibility. Particularly with print on demand, you can edit your book and make changes faster than a publisher who needs to shift an entire print run before edits can be made.
- You can go back and edit your book whenever you are ready.

The negatives:

- You're on your own - you have to figure this all out without the experience and support of a publisher behind you.
- There is no upfront monetary advance for your work, and you will also have to fund additional expenses such as cover design, proofreading and editing.
- It may be more difficult to get your book onto the shelves of a real-life bookshop.
- Some people do not take self-published books seriously, due to the existence of some poor-quality books letting the side down. Some people can overlook this, and read each new book on its merit, while others may have more reticence.
- You will be entirely responsible for marketing and promoting your book, and you will lack the contacts that a publisher usually has to get your book noticed.

A cautionary note on royalties however. The US Author's Guild[1] notes that self-published authors typically make half the overall royalties of authors published by a publishing company, despite typically having a vastly larger royalty percentage. This is likely skewed by anybody being

---

1 Authors Guild Survey Shows Drastic 42 Percent Decline in Authors Earnings in Last Decade. Accessed via https://www.authorsguild.org/industry-advocacy/authors-guild-survey-shows-drastic-42-percent-decline-in-authors-earnings-in-last-decade

able to self-publish a book and therefore some self-published book sales being very low. The sales goals of published versus self-published authors may also differ in that some self-publishing may simply be about getting a book out there rather than being motivated to sell lots of copies. However, it is also likely affected by some self-published authors simply not having the connections or publicity skills to promote their book. It's important to be honest with yourself when considering self-publishing - a publisher will invariably make more money than you in the long run from publishing your book. Will their knowledge and expertise help *you* make more money too?

If you decide to go down the self-publishing route, or simply want to know more about it, there are lots of free articles online or indeed books written about how to self-publish. If you decide that you want to pitch your book to a publisher, you then have the additional choice of deciding whether you are going to directly approach publishers yourself or work with an agent.

What about literary agents?

Some people choose to work with a literary agent who essentially acts as the bridge between an author and a publisher. Rather than directly submitting your proposal to a publisher you send it to an agent who forwards it to potential publishers on your behalf. They will have an excellent understanding of what different publishers are looking for and will work to secure you the best possible deal for your work. In return they receive commission from your royalties and any advance you receive. Typically this is around 15%. Be very wary of any agent that asks for payment in advance - this is unusual and may be indicative of someone taking advantage of new authors.

The benefits of working with an agent depend on your experience and predicted book sales. If you are confident in securing an excellent contract yourself you may decide you do not need the support of an agent, although do not underestimate the bonus of not having to discuss percentages and contracts with your publisher. Literary agents typically have numerous contacts and you may secure a publishing contract with a bigger publisher this way. Indeed, many publishing houses do not accept unsolicited manuscripts at all and liaise only with literary agents.

Remember agents only earn commission on your sales so will work to get you the best possible deal.

Once a literary agent has secured your publishing contract, they will also work with you to develop your book and be intimately involved in the construction of your manuscript - after all their reputation is on the line, along with yours! This can be really useful in helping develop your ideas and help you to submit the best possible version of your proposal.

You need to be realistic. If your book is unlikely to have a large audience, then you may not benefit from this added support. It is also possible that an agent will not be willing to work with you. Unless they are just starting out they are likely to be inundated with requests and are going to pick the books that will bring them the most revenue in return. They will also have carefully honed reputations with the big publishers and will likely have a certain standard of work that they will accept (by this read projected book sales).

Remember, if an agent does not accept you it's not that your work is necessarily poor quality, just that it may not create enough sales for them to benefit. If your book leads to £3000 of royalties per year (which is actually a good sales figure for less experienced authors) they will only receive around £450 for a considerable amount of work and expenses.

If you are interested in working with an agent you will need to find out as much about the agent you intend to approach as possible, write a book proposal, as well as a carefully crafted cover letter. Literary agents often have a niche interest or specialty and look specifically to represent authors whose work they genuinely believe in. It is essential that you send your proposal to an agent who is likely to be interested in your work. Sending your book on historical politics is unlikely to appeal to an agent who specialises in medical memoirs or children's books.

A practical tip is to look up literary agents and start by reading their biographies. They are sometimes cryptic and often do not give a lot away - because they expect you to do your homework. Find out what books they like to read (and read them), learn which books they have brought to publication, and what their interests are. When you have found some agents who you would love to represent you, check what they expect from you. Different literary agencies may require slightly different proposals, so again do your homework here.

Some tips for your cover letter:

- Check that the agent is currently open to submissions, and double check that your manuscript is a good fit for them. Sending irrelevant work is a waste of everyone's time.
- Always, always write your letter to a specific literary agent (not the agency), and it's usual to use their first name.
- Cover letters usually start with the line: "I am seeking representation for a non-fiction book titled:___"
- Your cover letter is the first (and may be the only) piece of your writing that the agent reads. Make every single word count.
- Keep your cover letter short - no more than one typed A4 page, and pay attention to your paragraphs and spacing to make it clean and easy on the eye.
- Expect to draft and redraft your cover letter to get it as good as you can. Remember that literary agents read for a living - check your work scrupulously, and ask someone with sharp eyes to do so too. It needs to be grammatically perfect, free from typos and formatting errors, and make sense.
- Provide a brief outline of your proposed book. This should be straight to the point avoiding any superfluous wording. Explain why your book is unique and why you are best qualified to write it.
- Explain why you think this particular agent is well placed to represent you - it must be personal. If you approach five agents, you will need to carefully edit your cover letter to be personal to each of those five different agents.
- You could include some personal details, such as which writers inspire you (bonus if the literary agent has the same taste in books), but don't include your life history.
- Do not email the same agent twice resubmitting your proposal - if they didn't like it the first time they probably won't like it the second time - unless you have substantially changed it.

One final word of warning is that literary agents may receive dozens of cover letters and book proposals each day. You may or may not receive an acknowledgement of yours. Some literary agencies have an online submission portal and these usually give an automated acknowledgement so you know your proposal is not lost in cyberspace. With other agencies, you will email the agent you are looking to represent you directly. They may or may not email you back to let you know. It's safe to say that if you have not heard within 6-8 weeks your proposal has probably not been accepted.

Finding the right publisher

If you have decided not to go down the agent route you will need to think about where to submit your proposal. Perhaps you have your heart set on a specific publisher, or maybe you have no idea where to start. If you are right at the beginning and wondering who's who in the field of publishing, then publishers fall into four main categories:

- Well known publishers who publish a broad range of topics (i.e. Penguin Random house, Harper Collins, Bloomsbury)
- Academic or education focussed (i.e. Macmillan, Pearson Education, Oxford University press, Springer, Routledge)
- Specialist (often very niche) or independent (tend to be smaller, may be specialist or may publish a wide range)
- Predatory (i.e. will charge you to publish your work)

These days you can find long lists of potential publishers online. Another great resource to get your hands on though is the Writers' & Artists' Yearbook, which is frequently updated. This book contains invaluable information on many of the different publishers. It also has lots of details about elements of book publishing such as adapting your book for a screenplay, writing series for television, and writing specific books such as travel or romcoms. Ultimately, choosing where to pitch your book is a combination of your expertise, your preferences, and your book topic.

Big name publishers

As you might expect, the larger companies typically are choosier due to how many proposals they receive. Of course, some authors with no previous writing experience do have their proposal accepted by a well-known publisher, but most do not. This isn't to do with the quality of your book necessarily but more how well they think it will sell depending on its potential market and timing. This is partly because they have a much larger budget to recoup as more people will be involved in the production, promotion and sale of the book, and partly due to having a reputation to uphold publishing high quality work.

This isn't to say if they reject you that your book is not high quality, just that with an absence of record behind you they may fail to see that, or be wary of taking the risk. Of course there is certainly no harm in trying, but do go into it with realistic expectations.

Academic publishers

Often those from an academic background publish their first book with an academic publisher. After a decade or so in academia and a growing list of research articles to your name, it is common to think about taking the plunge in pitching your first book proposal to an academic publisher, particularly if you are working in humanities or social sciences. This may take the form of a monograph or as an editor of a book where others write the chapters.

This isn't to say non academics cannot pitch to academic publishers, just that these publishers tend to accept more formalised heavily referenced work. Books tend to be pitched at students and researchers rather than someone looking for some bedtime reading.

Academic publishing operates in a slightly different way to more mainstream publishing specifically in relation to the way your book is promoted and the royalties you receive. Always check whether the publisher plans to publish your book in paperback as well as hardback (and when). It is common for academic publishers to only (or at least primarily) publish in hardback form, selling these copies at a great expense to libraries. This means that a) you will sell relatively few copies (a few hundred hardback copies is considered brilliant) and b) you will receive relatively little in royalties for your work (8 - 10% of a small figure is not very much at all).

This doesn't necessarily make academic publishing a no. After all there are many reasons to publish and if you are working in academia there is a certain prestige to having an academic publisher. Some fields may only consider this type of book 'real publishing' or, in other words, what they look to for promotion or research quality exercises. Often your audience may primarily be other academics, or you want to see your work published alongside your peers. It is worth taking a moment to consider whether your book has wider appeal to the public.

If you are reading this as an academic, you might be looking confused at this point. Someone will pay *me*? For publishing? Yes, this can be a shock. For an occupation where it is so common to not receive any money for your published research papers (or indeed paying to make them open access so that people can read them), hearing that you would receive any money at all for something that you write could blindside you enough not to care how many copies you sell. It could be, of course, that you are happy with simply seeing your book in print and having a book to your name. But do consider the alternative options.

If you do go for an academic publisher ask whether they plan to publish a paperback copy. This can make all the difference to your sales, reach and royalties. For example, Amy has an academic text published with Routledge. The hardback copy is priced at £150. No one buys that unless they're a library. However, the paperback version costs £30 and is often on offer. Unsurprisingly more people buy that version which amounts to more books being sold, more people actually reading what was written, and more royalties being earned.

Also ask them when they will publish your paperback version. Some will release hardback and paperback copies at the same time (we like these people). Others will wait a year or more to publish the paperback because they want to sell as many copies of the hardback as possible. Why? Because quite simply academic publishers make a lot of money out of hardback sales. If your typical academic gets around 10% of that sale and the book costs a few pounds to print, you can see why the companies like hardbacks that cost over £100. This money pays for everyone involved in publishing the book. We will leave it up to you to decide if it is fair that the author receives a relatively small amount of that sale.

Only you will know the answer to whether you will be better off with an academic or mainstream publisher. There is no one right answer for everyone, or indeed every book that you write. Are you aiming for your book to be on the shelves in academic libraries and bookshops and to be shared amongst your peers? Or do you want it to be on the shelves in your local high street and read by the general public? Of course, some of the most successful or influential books might be read by both audiences but who do you want to pitch the style, content and key messages to most? There lies your answer.

Specialist or independent publishers

As their name suggests, specialist publishers typically take on very specialist proposals. Take Persephone books for example – named by the Observer newspaper as one of the UKs top 50 independent shops. Persephone are probably not going to publish you, not because of the quality of your proposal but because they reprint neglected (or in other words out of print) books mostly by women writers and mostly from the interwar twentieth century period. However, if you are reading this as a 110-year-old woman whose book published in 1935 is no longer in print, you can suggest it being reborn on their website.

One of the benefits of pitching your work to independent, smaller publishers is that they may be more likely to work with you as a new writer. They may also have a more one to one or personal approach because they are a smaller company. It can feel more like being part of a team or family. This can however be a good or bad thing depending on what you are looking for. A smaller company probably has a smaller team working to support your book development and promotion. They probably have a smaller marketing budget, and a smaller reach as a consequence. Having a niche book that a small publisher believes in wholeheartedly and gets to a small, but specific audience might be exactly what you need. On the other hand, having a book with wide appeal that is hard to get off the ground due to marketing budget constraints might feel frustrating.

Independent (indie) publishers may publish a wide range of books, or they may specialise in a particular field or genre. It's worth looking at what other type of books the publisher you are considering pitching your book to end up publishing. Would your book fit in well within the other books available? Does it fit the general vibe? Independent publishers may be an excellent fit if your book gels well within their range, but your proposal is likely to be turned away if it doesn't fit their ethos.

Predatory book publishers

As an academic Amy is used to numerous emails, often daily, offering to publish her work rapidly in some obscure journal ... if she just hands over thousands of pounds. These journals typically have little reputation, peer review or standards but will publish anything for the right amount of money. The growing pressure on academics to publish has enabled their growth. Although awareness is growing of these journals, what is less well known is that there is unfortunately also a rapidly expanding market for predatory book publishers.

These publishers either typically want to make money out of you without paying for your content or even take advantage of your desire to publish by charging *you*. Although you will end up with a published book (at a cost) it is unlikely that it will be well promoted or that you will be fairly treated. Avoid, unless your main goal is to have a book in print and aren't too fussed about sales, reputation or accessibility of the work.

Some ways to spot a likely predatory book publishing offer include:

- Has a publisher emailed you out of the blue wanting to publish your book – when you have no prior experience of writing and do not have a particularly big reputation in your field?
- Are they offering to publish you for free (but with no royalties) or worse still, charge you to publish?
- Have you ever heard of them before? Have you heard of any of the books or authors they have published?

Other factors to consider

Alongside considering the main approach of the different publishing types, when it comes to deciding which specific publisher you might ideally like to work with, it's worth considering some broader factors. Maybe you will just be thrilled to publish anywhere that would accept you for your debut book but over time, as the shine wears off, you might regret a rushed choice. Here are some things to think about:

- **What is the ethos of the publisher?** Do they value new writers and subjects that are important to you?
- **What is the reputation of the publisher?** How do readers view them? Are their authors happy?
- **What other topics have they published?** Do they limit themselves to certain categories? How will you feel if they suddenly publish something off-piste or that you eminently disagree with?
- **Who else do they publish?** Do they publish authors whose work or writing style you admire?

- **How large is the company?** Are you dealing with a giant or a one (wo)man band? How many people will make decisions on your book? On the one hand, multiple viewpoints can help shape your work and help challenge you; but too many cooks/editors can sometimes spoil the broth.
- **Who will you deal with on a day to day basis?** Will you know your editor and the people at the top? How do you feel about that?
- **Do you like the 'look' of their books?** We know you should never judge a book by its cover but equally covers matter. What say, if any, will you have over cover design and title?
- **Where and how do they promote their work?** Have you seen the publishers and their books promoted in the press? Do they have a good social media presence? Do they actively encourage and support their authors to promote their work?

Ultimately we all hope that our dream publisher selects our work the first time we submit it. Pragmatically you may have to be flexible in your criteria although it is always worth reflecting on the question: what is more important to you - your desired publisher or speed of publishing? Again, there's no right answer to that. Try reflecting on it from both sides. How might it feel to delay or re-edit versus publishing somewhere else?

Dealing with rejection

It is likely that at some point, depending on who you are pitching your idea to, you will get a book proposal rejected. Unless you are solely self-publishing, as soon as you put your book idea out there to an agent or publisher then someone along that decision making chain (and there may be many of them) can say no. We'd go so far as to say that you should probably go into proposing your book with the assumption that there will be a no at some point. This isn't pessimistic thinking or a glass half full approach, but rather it's a pragmatic and realistic one. So many of the big-name authors got rejected at some point. It's just that rather than giving up they learned from that experience, picked themselves up, made the necessary changes and tried again.

Indeed, as a positive bedtime story interlude here, Amy had her first book proposal royally rejected. It got quite high up the chain of approval at a big publishing company and was then ceremoniously rejected with the statement that it wouldn't appeal to a big enough audience. To be fair she spent a good couple of days wallowing in the absolute knowledge that she could not write and would never, ever be a published author (like, *ever*) before dusting herself off, sending off her proposal to a better fit and proceeding to publish ten books within five years. She feels that on balance she's just about made her point now that she can publish a book, although some days she's not sure.

Being rejected naturally hurts and there is no one correct reaction to the experience. You might be the sort of person to bounce back immediately, see it as fate and as an opportunity to hone your idea or go in a different direction. You may also feel hurt, angry, or like a complete failure – or all three at once. Feeling this way is absolutely normal and, in fact, probably a better reaction than pushing it all down inside you never to be dwelled on again. It makes you human. It's what you do next that matters. Are you going to sulk and let one rejection beat you? Or are you going to get back up again, dust yourself (and your proposal) off and try again?

Top tip here – burying emotions never works in the long term. If you are feeling hurt it's worth a) taking the time to work out what emotions you are feeling b) reflecting on why you feel that way and c) giving yourself some set time to process it. If you are feeling negatively, can you identify how you are feeling? Is it anger? Like you've been scorned? Rejected? Worrying you're a failure? Anxiety over time passing? These are all natural things to feel. It is worth thinking about why you are feeling this way. Is it just a natural reaction to getting your hopes up and someone saying no? Or is it triggering a memory from your past?

- Maybe a previous partner told you that you'd never do anything worthwhile
- Or your parents praised your sibling as the one who achieves good things
- Or you still have a bone to pick with that teacher who told you that you'd never be good at X/Y/Z

Even though your brain is screaming at you that the two things are linked and pressing all those horrible buttons of shame and anger, this isn't anything to do with them. They weren't right. And publishing is a really tough gig. The growth of self-publishing (a good thing in itself) has led to the belief that being able to publish a book is just an everyday thing to do, rather than recognising it in the same way we think about marathons / PhDs / MasterChef-level cooking. There are some AMAZING self-published books out there but self-publishing is a wholly different experience than having to be accepted by a publisher. It removes the rejection (and in *some* cases, let's be honest, the quality checks). Do not compare yourself to this. And remember to check out Chapter eight on impostor syndrome later in the book.

It can also be worth taking some time to allow yourself to wallow. However, put a deadline on it. Maybe you want to take a day. Or a week. Moan away. Hate the universe. Tell everyone just how wrong they were. Then, when the time's up, get on with it. Forward facing only. What's the next step in getting your publishing dream realised? Read any feedback with a clear head rather than potentially negatively exaggerating any constructive criticism in the midst of the initial disappointment.

An important point to remember here is that a rejection absolutely does not mean that you are a terrible writer with a terribly written proposal for a terrible book idea. It just means that either the proposal isn't quite ready yet, it's not a good match for the publisher, or is simply the wrong time. All of those are fixable, with a different approach, or time and some more work. Be honest – do you think the proposal needs more work? Do you need more development as a writer before launching this book?

If you fall into this category or fear that you do, then there is hopefully lots of good advice in the rest of this book for you. Practice (and perseverance) really does make perfect – or as close to perfect as you need to be. Do you have a trusted friend that you can ask to read your sample chapter or proposal? Would you benefit from working with an agent if you're not already doing so? Hey, we never said this was going to be easy – but we do know how you feel.

However, it also is possible that it's not you – it's them. This isn't because the publishers are simply insane not to see your talent but rather for reasons to do with their business. Maybe it wasn't the right fit. Maybe they already have other leading books on this topic, or someone else just submitted a similar proposal. Maybe they are focussing elsewhere right now, or taking a different direction.

They may also simply be too busy – perhaps they have taken on a lot of authors recently or had an unexpected (or more than expected) success and have temporarily outgrown themselves. Things like Brexit and Covid-19 have also put strain on smaller publishers with all the additional paperwork and regulations. If the publisher responds to say 'no thanks' do ask them for some simple feedback if they can spare the time. Additionally, if you don't hear from them, don't automatically assume they wish to forget all about you as your idea was so rubbish. They could just be inundated and can't reply to everyone who submits.

It also doesn't mean that your book itself isn't good. It could simply be a case of your area of expertise being very competitive. Your book idea may be brilliant, it just might be that there are more developed and experienced authors also pitching books at this time. This is why it is a good idea to not have your heart set only on one publisher but rather a range of options. Make that list – your absolute favourite, followed by others you would consider and work your way down (though maybe don't tell the ones at the 'bottom' that they were your last preference). This is where an agent can be really helpful again in supporting you in pitching to the best possible fit for you, and helping you manage and work out the next steps in your pitching.

If you get to the bottom of your potential publisher list without a positive response, it might be time to consider whether a) more work needs to be done on your proposal and / or b) whether you might want to consider self-publishing this book. Only you will really know the answer to this one. If you have no previous expertise in publication and have honed your idea as much as you feel that you can, you might decide that self-publishing is the way forward for you right now. Remember you can always make a different decision for the next book.

Chapter 5

Writing a book proposal

If you're hoping to have your book published by a publishing company, it is likely that you will need to write a book proposal for them. Occasionally some agencies will not require an extensive proposal, but this typically only happens if you already have a lot of writing experience and / or are very well known outside your immediate circles for the topic you will be writing about. Even in those cases it is still likely that they want to see a book outline which describes the content and structure of the book.

Alternatively, some publishers actually prefer a finished manuscript - especially if you are a new author. Even then it is still likely that you will need to provide an overview so that they can decide whether to spend considerable time reading your manuscript. What we're really saying is that no matter how much of the book your publisher expects to see written, you are very likely to need to produce a book proposal.

A book proposal can also be helpful for you because it can help clarify the overall structure and length of the book in *your* head. You may have a clear idea of what your book will look like, but you might just have the broad topic and aims in mind. Breaking it down into smaller chunks by creating a chapter structure and estimated word count can help to guide you in your writing too.

Bear in mind that different people might read your book proposal. It could be read only by your agent or someone at the publishing company. However, some publishers send out proposals for review. They take this really seriously, paying the reviewers (typically subject specialists in academia or practice) in either money or free books to write detailed reviews. Always plan for this happening because thinking about who is likely to read it can help shape and strengthen your proposal. In other words, don't leave out all references to the author or researcher you perceive to be competition as there is a real chance they may end up reviewing your book.

So, what does a book proposal look like? Essentially it is your chance to persuade a publishing agency that your book is worth them putting their effort into publishing it. Different agencies may have different preferred formats (check on their website; or if you are using a publicist, with them for preferred format). It is possible you may have to write slightly different versions for different companies. However typical sections include:

Synopsis

This is essentially an overview of what your book is about and why it should be published. It is usually fairly short, perhaps 300 - 500 words, and is one of the most important parts of a proposal because it might be the only part an agency actually reads. Although it is usually at the start of the proposal, it can help to write this last, once you have all the finer details worked out in your head (and on paper).

Your synopsis should be bold, yet still factual. What is the key message of your book? What is it about? Why is it important to write about that? Why is it a priority to publish now - is it topical and timely, or is it a topic that is always going to be of interest regardless of what is currently in the news? It can also help to add here who the intended audience is and why you are the best person to write this book.

This is not the place to be wordy. You should be as to the point as possible, bringing your key points to the reader. It can help to write the synopsis in short paragraphs or bullet points, each with its own key point. Although this is only a short part of your proposal, the need for it to be polished and hard hitting can mean that it takes the longest to write. Give it the time it deserves.

Novelty or main selling points

Here you would write about your books 'best bits' or what makes it a unique and attractive proposition for a publisher to invest in. This part should be snappy and to the point. Using bullet points of no more than around 50 – 75 words can help. You might like to think about:

- Why is this particular book important?
- Why is now the right time for it to be published?
- What gap in the market / topical subject does your book meet?
- How is your book different from other similar books?
- Who will read this book?
- Why are you the best person to write it?
- Why is the publisher the right home for it?

Main competition

Often publishers will want to know what other work has been published in this area, when and how it is priced. This one is a fine balance. On the one hand you really want to sell the novelty of your work. You need to be clear how your book fills a gap in what has already been published and complements others in this area. You can use the success of similar books to your advantage – have they sold well? Then it's likely that your book on a similar topic might too.

This, however, is a key point to stop and reflect. How similar is your book to what has already been published? Is there a genuine gap or alternative market? Does the world need another book on the same topic? Most hopefully yes it does but this is a useful step in making sure that your book is genuinely novel and not at risk of being accused of being a copy of someone else's work.

On the other side of this argument you might find yourself unable to list any truly competitive books. This might feel like a positive, which it is to some extent. However you also don't want to make out that your idea is so novel that the topic appears obscure. Always make sure that you have searched for similar books even if you have not come across them until this point because if you leave out books that everyone else is aware of, this might make you look like you don't know the topic well at all.

If nothing has genuinely been published in this area, present your case for why this has not previously happened and why it is the right time to launch a book on this topic. Is it because the topic itself is novel i.e. in response to something like Covid-19 or a recent event? Or is it because there has been a lack of awareness for this topic until recently?

Finally, don't be tempted to try and ignore the competition. If you leave out popular books closely related to your topic area because you're worried that the publisher will think yours isn't good enough, then that could backfire. You might get away with it if they don't realise - but if they don't realise, do you then really want them publishing your book on this topic? It's a double-edged sword. Also remember that you might have your proposal sent out to someone whose seminal book you have ignored. Once your book is in the public domain, if you've claimed that your book is entirely novel and it is not, then authors could be, shall we say, displeased. Hell hath no fury like an author ignored!

Book structure

Publishers would like to see an overview of what your book will look like. This is often best presented in a table split into chapter headings, description and approximate word count. Writing this section can be useful in getting your head around your overall book structure and aims if you haven't fully worked this out already. Here's an example of what this might look like (guess the time of year it was when Amy was putting together this chapter):

Chapter	**Description**	**Word count**
The joy of trees	A history of Christmas trees including the varied cultural and social reasons why people bring trees into their homes at Christmas	3500
Picking a Christmas tree	Types of Christmas tree, locations on where to buy Christmas trees, and personal preferences	2500
Buying decorations	Historical and cultural influences on tree decorations; trends in tree decoration; colour scheme decisions; modern versus heirloom considerations	3500

Author biography

This section is your chance to tell the agent, or publisher all about why you are the best person to write this book. Useful information for this section may include:

- **Any current (or previous) education, employment or work experiences** that are relative to the topic of your book or offer broader experience of writing. For example, you might include your experience of working in healthcare for a book that was related to healthcare, but you might also want to talk about experience of writing or publication in any of your roles i.e. in academia, journalism, or editing. Include both paid and voluntary positions.

- **Previous publications** including books, but also formats such as academic journals, writing for the media, and blogging. Essentially, what is your experience of writing and sharing it with others? Data such as any awards won, significant readership figures, or other accolades could be included here.

- **Social media and other connections** – here you might like to include information about how well known you are as an expert in your subject area. Bluntly - social media and other connections help to sell books (more on this in Chapter 14). How well known you are to others in terms of how much they trust you, and perceive you as an expert on your subject area, can make a real boost to the saleability of your book. Publishers love authors with good social media connections as it makes promoting books easier.

- **The personal touch** – it can help to finish off with a simple line about yourself to add the personal touch to the proposal. We don't mean tell everyone about your childhood swimming badges (well unless the book is about swimming) but more a simple line contextualising yourself within this proposal. Something like 'Jenna lives in picturesque but rainy Cornwall with her two children and dog Max'.

Every author bio will be slightly different but here is an example of what a strong bio might look like:

> Natalie has over 20 years working with pregnant and new families as a community midwife in South London. Her passion for running antenatal hypnobirthing classes led to her wanting to distil her experience of working with hundreds of families into this modern guide to hypnobirthing. **[*This paragraph brings together Natalie's key strengths and experience in relation to her book proposal.*]**

Natalie has previously written about her knowledge and experience of supporting parents with antenatal education in several publications. In 2020 she was invited to write an article in 'The Practising Midwife' journal about the benefits of hypnobirthing. She has also contributed to a feature article in the Daily Mail exploring what hypnobirthing is and how families could benefit from it. In 2019 Natalie was also a clinical member of a research team who conducted a study into parents experiences of hypnobirthing. The findings from this study were published in the journal 'Midwifery'. **[*This paragraph focuses on Natalie's writing experience, giving details that show she has experience of writing, including for different audiences.]***

Alongside her clinical work Natalie runs a popular social media page 'Hypnobirthing and You' which has over 10,000 followers on both Instagram and Facebook. As part of this she is a regular blogger and has also recorded two podcasts about hypnobirthing and antenatal preparation. **[*This paragraph highlights how Natalie's work has a strong following and she is skilled at, and willing to engage in, different forms of social media promotion.*]**

It is not essential that you have lots of experience in each of these areas for your book proposal to be accepted, but if you do have experience it helps to highlight it. However do remember that your experience is only part of the overall proposal. A publisher might see something special in your idea and be willing to take a more novice writer on, especially if you can show that your writing is of a good standard through a completed sample chapter (more on this coming up).

Do I need to have written any of the book for a proposal to be accepted?

This really does depend on your experience as an author and the preferences of the publishing company that you are submitting to. Some companies might prefer you to have written the entire book in the first place (although others would prefer to have some say in forming the structure and focus of the book). Many would like to see a sample chapter of your book, particularly if you have no previous writing experience. This may change as you become more established, especially if you can simply refer them to your sales figures.

What should a sample chapter look like? Again, some publishers might have a preference here but if you are able to choose, choose the chapter that will likely make the best lasting impression. Sometimes this could be the introduction if it really helps set the scene and importance of the book. Often it isn't though – it's one of the chapters somewhere else in your book, probably nowhere near the beginning. You might choose the chapter that is most topical right now, one that you know best (or have the most experience around), or one that is a topic that will draw in readers, maybe even with a controversial subject topic.

As an example, when Amy wrote the proposal for her first book 'Breastfeeding Uncovered' which explores all the different psychological, social and cultural influences on infant feeding she chose the chapter that looked at societal attitudes to breastfeeding in public. She chose this because a) she had already recently written about this topic in some research papers so had a head start on the background research; b) it had some eye opening statistics in it to pique interest; c) there had been a number of recent media headlines about the topic; and d) because the ridiculous nature of some of the research findings on the topic allowed her to showcase different forms of writing style such as humour.

Writing a sample chapter can feel more challenging than writing other parts of the book. You're obviously eager to impress and showcase your knowledge and talents but also it can sometimes be a difficult task to write a stand-alone completed chapter of a book. Although some authors tend to tackle one chapter from start to finish at a time (Lyndsey in our case), others take a far more scattergun approach to it, jumping from chapter to chapter gradually building up a book rather than one chapter at a time (that would be Amy here). Even if you do take the first approach you will most likely find that when you write further chapters, you'll go back to the previous chapters to add in related information or link to different aspects. Remember this chapter is still a work in progress when you return to write the full book.

Do take your time over this chapter and spend more time on it than you likely will the other chapters in the book, particularly if you're trying to impress a selective publishing company or have no previous experience of publishing. Publishers want to know that you can write. Yes, they can edit your work (and likely will do) but they need you to show that you have a high standard of writing to begin with. The only time this doesn't apply is when you're a celebrity or someone with extensive experience of your topic area and the publisher desperately wants your story or particularly unique (read best-selling) idea and probably plans to help you write it. In short, it's important that you really focus on polishing this chapter as much as possible.

It can be a good idea to share your sample chapter with some select others that you trust. Don't be tempted to send it only to people you know will love it because they love you, or the subject area, so much that they will literally like anything they read about it. Try giving it to someone who knows nothing about the subject area, or your friend who likes playing devil's advocate and will spot holes in your argument. Now is not the time to be fragile about feedback – it's best to get it now before you send it off to those with the real power. If you struggle with spelling or grammar, it might also be a good idea to have this chapter proofread by someone.

Essentially your sample chapter is you going on a first date with that person you've had your eye on for a long time - make sure you don't have spinach stuck in your teeth!

Chapter 6

Contracts, book sales and royalties

After the verbal (or more likely, emailed) agreement to publish your book, you will receive a written formal contract from your publisher. This essentially outlines firstly what your responsibilities as an author are, and secondly what your publisher's responsibilities to you are. Many are standard, but you should check the details of the following main areas:

- **Copyright**. Usually, as the author, you will own the copyright. This will often also include a clause about what to expect if your book is printed in other languages, and what the arrangements are if your book is made into a film.

- **Advance and royalties.** Details of the advance you will receive, and when, should be in your contract; as should the breakdown of royalties for hardback, paperback, audiobook and ebook. There may also be details of bonuses for appearing on a Bestseller list, winning a prize, or dramatisation of your book. This section should also tell you how and when your royalties will be paid.

- **Author discounts.** Most publishers sell author copies at a discounted rate, and this, as well as whether there are any clauses or conditions should be detailed. This might include where you are allowed to sell your book, for example whether you are allowed to set up a stall opposite your publisher at an event they regularly attend, and undercut them (spoiler - you're probably not).

- **Deadline.** The timescale should be clear in the contract so that everyone knows what timeframe they are working towards. This doesn't mean that there is no flexibility, but the intended date for you to hand over the manuscript should be obvious.

- **Editing and production.** Details of the editing process, and the publisher's role in organising this will be in your contract, as will who pays for what - typically, the publisher will pay for editing, proofreading, cover design, marketing, and all other associated costs, but do check.

- **Publication.** The intended publication date as well as the print run will be outlined. This is useful to know because if you want to fix a typo, you will usually only be able to do this after the first print run has sold, so keep track of minor edits / typos and these can usually be quickly changed before the next print run.

- **Advertising.** There is usually a section detailing what kind of publicity you can expect for your book. Note that unless your book is expected to sell very well, it is unlikely that this will be a world book tour! But it should include details of how many complimentary copies you will be provided with for advertising and promotional purposes.

- **Termination, violation of contract and out of print details.** If anything catastrophic happens this is the section that deals with the publisher failing to deliver on their side of the terms. Usually all rights revert to the author in this case.

- **Conflicts of interest and right of first refusal.** Some publishers have first refusal on a subsequent manuscript, although this is often felt to be too restrictive for some experts or academics who may publish extensively on a specialist topic. Sometimes this is limited to a certain time frame, or only the next book - just make sure you check.

Although they are mostly fairly standard, contracts can sometimes contain a fair amount of legal jargon, so if you're not sure what you're signing up for, ask for clarification, or seek independent advice.

How many copies will you sell?

A common question many authors or authors-to-be are keen to ask is how much money can they expect to make from their books? How many copies will they sell? The answer? Maybe loads. But unfortunately probably less than you think. Making a good guess is also really difficult. For a start, looking at 'average' book sales is pointless as it is skewed by the very few books that sell millions of copies. Different genres and types of books sell different amounts. Unfortunately quality is also not a good predictor. There are many books with *very* high sales that have no evidence base whatsoever and some highly accurate ones based on decades of academic work that have sold a few hundred copies (if that).

Even books shortlisted for prizes such as the Man Booker don't always sell that many copies - with some selling just a few thousand copies. Quantity of sales and quality of book should not be equated!

Translating that to real sales, a figure that is often stated is '3000 copies' for nonfiction. For self-published authors this drops to 250 copies. This would roughly fit with median author's earnings (details coming up). Be aware that those figures will a) be skewed as above; b) aren't clear in terms of time since publication; and c) don't appear to have reliable sources behind them. Of course, books that sell well are by their very nature more visible. We see them talked about and on the shelves in the local supermarket. It can make high book sales seem more common than they really are. But for every book like this you would find many more that sell just a few hundred in their lifetime. The real question for you is - does this matter?

Reflecting back for a moment on the 'why write a book' chapter, remember that book sales are only a small reflection of your books worth. Yes of course earning money from writing is nice and selling lots of books is a wonderful feeling. However, actually getting an email from someone you have helped is pretty nice too. As is seeing your work used in teaching. Or recommended on social media. Books also lead to other, sometimes paid, opportunities such as speaking about your work - or may increase the number of clients you attract or the impact of your research. None of that is reflected in a book sales figure.

Finding out how many copies you have sold is harder than you might expect. Publishers will typically send you a retrospective royalty statement listing sales twice a year, or you will be able to keep track of this on different platforms if you are self-published. Publishers might give you more frequent data if you have a genuine need and ask nicely but harassing them frequently is unlikely to end well. You can also make a vague guess from Amazon book rankings although this helps more with keeping track of your overall pattern of sales than it does accurate figures as no one really seems to know what the Amazon sales ranking translates to. Nielson BookScan gives accurate figures but costs A LOT of money, so typically only larger publishers will subscribe. You can sign up sometimes through Amazon marketplace for the 'bargain' individual subscriber figure of approximately $2500.

Book Royalties

As noted above, a typical book royalty figure will be around 8-10% of a book's RRP. Audio and e-book sales are likely to attract different rates as there are typically less production costs involved. The rate you are offered will vary between publishers and may be variable dependent on your expertise. Some publishers will offer a flat rate per first batch of books sold (e.g. 5000 copies), rising as sales grow and initial production costs have been covered. You may be able to negotiate this but again think about your true bargaining power before suggesting wild figures. There's an important line between knowing your own worth and appearing wildly unprofessional in demanding large sums for a first book on a niche subject.

Book royalties are typically a small part of RRP and much lower than you might receive percentage wise compared to self-publishing. Bear in mind that although you are the one doing the writing, remember that the publisher has considerable costs too. They will be covering the cost and labour of:

- Reading and commenting on your book proposal
- Editing and proofreading
- Indexing your book
- Cover design and blurb
- Book layout
- Liaising with book sellers
- Printing and storage
- Press releases and media promotion
- Dealing with any criticism / errors in your work
- Selling your book at book fairs and conferences
- Providing expertise and emotional support

All of these costs add up and although they may appear to make a much, much larger profit on your book than you do it is probably smaller than you think. They are also taking a risk by publishing your work as they need to pay in advance of receiving any sales at all to get your book on the shelves. Don't forget that you are paying for their expertise and reputation too. Unless they are a brand-new publisher they have spent a lot of time and money honing their skills, just as you have as a writer.

In terms of how much money you can expect to make from a book, that really does depend on your subject area, your skill as an author and your publishers reach. Unfortunately it is unlikely, at least with your first few books, that you are going to make enough money to give up your day job (unless you happen to have a lot of savings, a very supportive partner or live very frugally in a tent).

Two surveys that examine the income for authors show sobering results. The Author's Guild conducts a regular Author Income Survey[2], which explores the writing-related income of American authors. The last survey of 5,067 was published in 2018. In the UK the Author's Licensing and Collecting Society (ALCS) commissioned the UK Copyright and Creative Economy Centre at the University of Glasgow to write a report on over 50,000 writer's earnings, which was published in 2019[3]. The reports include sales from books alone and a broader income figure from writing - such as speaking opportunities, commissioned articles based on their books and so forth.

An important point to consider is that both reports use the median (the middle figure) not the mean (overall average) because the large earnings of a small minority of authors would hugely skew the data. Typically mean earnings are three times that of median earnings, with some huge figures included. A minority of authors are earning A LOT of money from writing whereas, unfortunately, many authors are earning very, very little from their writing (and sometimes nothing at all). Also remember that these figures are based on overall earnings and not earnings per book. If you have five books published you might expect to earn more than someone with just one - although not necessarily if their book has a wider reach.

Overall, both reports show similar earnings and neither are overwhelmingly positive if you are hoping to make huge sums from your writing. In the US report the median earnings for full time writers was $20,300 and in the UK it was £10,497. In both cases this had dropped by around 40% over the last decade or so. When part time writers were taken into consideration that median US income dropped to $6,080 and

---

2 https://www.authorsguild.org/industry-advocacy/authors-guild-survey-shows-drastic-42-percent-decline-in-authors-earnings-in-last-decade/

3https://www.societyofauthors.org/News/News/2019/May/Report-on-authors-earnings-diversity-implications

UK to £3000. A lot of profit emerged from associated engagements rather than book sales, with a mean US book sale royalty figure of $3,100. However you look at the data the median income is far less than the poverty line if you are supporting a family.

The ALCS survey notes that this includes significant variation in income with the top 10% of writers taking home approximately 70% of all earnings. Predictably and disappointingly, the majority of respondents in the ALCS data are White (94%) and female authors earn three quarters of the income that male authors do. Earnings also peak in the 35 - 44 year age category, declining with age although this may reflect intensity of writing. Finally, although authors themselves are not earning a lot of money, notably the mean household income for full time authors was £81,000 (median £50,000) suggesting that many are heavily supported financially by a higher earning partner. In the ALCS survey 70% of respondents stated that they had to also earn money from other sources.

It's worth noting here that you can sign up as an author in the UK to the Public Lending Right (PLR) scheme administered by the British Library. You will receive a very small amount of royalties (currently around 11p) each time one of your books is borrowed from a library. This all adds up and the scheme is free to join. Find out more at https://www.bl.uk/plr.

You can also sign up to the Authors Licensing and Collecting Agency which helps collect money for authors (of all different types of work including journal articles, scripts and magazine pieces) when their work is photocopied, scanned or digitally reused, or in some cases lent by a library overseas. Find out more here https://www.alcs.co.uk .

Advances on royalties

Sometimes you may be offered an advance for your work. Going back to our romantic image earlier in the book of how we might envisage the writing experience to look, you might be expecting this to be a big cash advance to support you in writing your book. Unfortunately this is probably unlikely to be the case the first time you write a book, unless you have a truly brilliant idea and a fantastic agent - or happen to be Michelle or Barack Obama who reportedly secured $60 million for a two book deal.

Overall, the ALCS report above found that 69% of those who describe themselves as full time authors received an advance for their work.

However this is likely skewed by the fact that they are full time authors - which came first? The full time writing or the advance which enabled them to become a full-time writer? It also depends on the type of publisher you are submitting to. Larger publishers are more likely to offer you an advance (and a bigger one) whereas advances in academic publishing are practically unheard of.

Getting an advance is obviously a lovely thing - who wouldn't want to receive money in advance of actually having done very much? And get paid to spend their days writing? Do go ahead and pop the champagne, but remember that an advance of £1000 means that you won't receive any more money until your book has generated more than £1000 worth of royalties. However for many newer authors who are writing alongside their other commitments, receiving an advance is a brilliant psychological boost as it shows someone is prepared to invest in your writing, even if it is just £500.

In terms of how much of an advance you can expect, be realistic. If your publisher does provide advances then numerous factors will determine how much. Smaller companies may not have the cash flow to invest in large advances no matter how well they think your book will sell. The size of the advance may also reflect your experience and reputation. The publisher is essentially betting on the success of your work. It is an investment. How quickly will they recoup their money? Understandably if you've never published before then they will be taking more of a risk. However if you've got a number of book successes behind you then this figure is likely to rise. If you get to the stage of having sold tens of thousands of copies of a book, it's probably time to think about an agent to help negotiate a better deal for the future.

If you cannot secure an advance but have secured a book deal, it can help psychologically to think of this as a sort of advance and validation of your work. After all, they are prepared to stump up their money and expertise to get your book to print. Depending on the publisher this is effectively investing thousands of pounds (or even more) in your work.

Chapter 7

Finding time to write

At some point, all the pondering and thinking about your book has to turn into getting the book written. This might sound obvious, but most writers have busy lives and therefore getting words down can feel daunting. You may be able to carve out some protected time to write, but it's a reality that you may be having to think of ways to be efficient with your writing. This chapter has lots of ideas for helping you to identify when you might get your book written. Make sure you leave enough time for editing - we have lots of practical hints and tips for editing your work in Chapter 12.

'How do you find the time to write?' has to be one of the most common questions we are both asked. People often have very fixed ideas of how long it takes to write a book (often a year it seems) and how writing must happen (such as formally sitting at a desk, or writing at set times per day). Going back to that initial image of 'the writer' at the start of the book – what preconceived ideas do you hold?

The truth is that there are as many different ways to write as there are writers and what works for you will depend on your other responsibilities, timescale and indeed personality. For example the idea of sitting down in a structured way to write horrifies Amy whereas Lyndsey prefers to ringfence time in her diary, knowing that otherwise she will fall foul of the tendency to say 'yes' to doing other things when she really should be writing.

When it comes to actually getting words down on paper, everyone writes in their own way. You might not know how you write best when you first get started, so be patient with yourself. You may need to try out several ways of writing and see which option works for you – asking around and finding out what works well for another writer may not necessarily be helpful.

Know your most creative time

One of the most helpful writers' tools is to know what time of day, or which circumstances lead to more productive writing. You might already have a sneaky suspicion that because you're a night owl, your most productive time is late afternoon, or evening. Or perhaps you know you're an early bird and therefore if it's going to get done at all, it has to be before lunchtime. Trying to fight your natural circadian rhythm over this isn't likely to end well. Some people, like Cinderella, turn into the proverbial pumpkin past a certain time of night, whereas others write best late in the afternoon and into the evening. Conversely, some people might find this differs day by day. Sometimes you face weeks of barely being able to write past midday and then suddenly one day nothing can stop you working into the small hours of the morning.

Expect some periods of procrastination

We have never heard of anyone who doesn't have 'off days', or days when they mess around on social media, clean the house, do a hundred random jobs and then finally, eight hours later, sit and stare at a blank screen. We all do it. It's normal. It is quite amazing how much funny stuff you can find on the internet when there's a book to write. We would probably go as far as to say that you should probably build 'messing about' time into your writing plans.

If you're anything like either of us, you might find that the closer you get to your deadline the more the urge to procrastinate starts to slip away. Some people simply need the time pressure to help motivate them - many people refer to this as 'the fear'. As you grow more experienced as a writer you may be able to factor this more intense productivity, driven by fear, into your writing timetable; although it's a strategy that obviously carries risks if you have a fixed deadline.

Sometimes though, procrastination isn't really procrastination. You don't have to be sitting at your desk to be legitimately working on your book. You might actually do some of the best work on your book when you're not writing. Perhaps you will think about the concepts in your book as you vacuum, or as you clear your mind when swimming or on a long walk, something you have been struggling with for weeks suddenly becomes clearer.

Downtime is important too. Think of your brain like a muscle. We can't force it to work all the time - like aching muscles after a workout your mind will benefit from periods of rest too. If you are really struggling with procrastination or writer's block, give yourself permission to have a break. You might just find you come back to writing much more motivated and find that the words flow again.

Making your writing sustainable

It can be helpful for some people to develop a simple routine for writing. If you're someone whose brain finds comfort in the familiar routines you incorporate into your day, then you may find it helpful to build these in. Some of us are more susceptible to breaks in routine or pattern than others. For example, generally Lyndsey can be very flexible though she occasionally gets rattled if some parts of her day are disrupted.

If you know that this is your tendency as well, try to anticipate this as a barrier to writing productively and create a predictable time when you know you will write, based on where you work best, and the time of day you work best. Even if this is simply making a cup of coffee and turning off screens so that you can concentrate. During the Covid-19 pandemic and subsequent lockdowns when nobody had the house to themselves, many people came up with a system where they would make a sign for the door so that their kids knew they were writing.

Some people find it helpful to have a designated space to write in. Not everyone has the luxury of an office space to work in. But we have seen some amazingly designed corners in living spaces which can create a feeling of a space to think and work. For many people, an uncluttered desk is a must, otherwise this can lead to distraction and some of us (ahem!) decide that now is the perfect and obvious time to have a major tidy up. For other people, having silence, or some quiet music helps. Try to be disciplined about turning your phone upside down, or leaving it in another room so you can't be diverted to some social media storm in a teacup that will take your focus away from what you're writing.

Make sure you don't overcommit while you're working on a book. At the time of writing this, Lyndsey is also trying to plan another book, do a research project, and she's still fiddling with two other books that can't quite be sent for editing yet. Amy refused to provide a comment when asked about overcommitment. Definitely do as we suggest, rather than what we do. However, we believe this makes us brilliantly qualified to caution you of the dangers of over-commitment. Before you turn into a grouchy, fire-breathing book monster, learn the wonderful and under-appreciated art of saying 'No'. Game-changer!

The reality is that life doesn't stop while you write. The world will keep spinning just as fast as it always has done, and you will get asked to do things, roped into jobs and find yourself juggling. So you may have to be intentional and selective about the extra tasks you take on. Book writing isn't just about the time it actually takes to type. It's also about the research you will need to do, the fact-checking, the groundwork, and the headspace while you organise your thoughts.

Ad hoc brilliance

As much as we would like to think that we are in control of our writing, much of your writing will come as the result of an epiphany that you have while making dinner, in the bath, feeding the cat, or doing the school run. It would be nice if we could turn on creative inspiration and genius when we were sitting at our desks, ready to write. But sadly, for some reason, this is often not the way it works.

We both now come to expect that we will have a flash of insight or a lightbulb moment when we don't necessarily expect it. This is not always convenient. Your brain is busy rifling through the filing cabinet of your mind, and linking concepts together while you're not aware of it. It doesn't know that driving at 70mph is not a great moment to suddenly make a connection that brings together your entire chapter. Lyndsey has been known to pull over so she can write something down, or suddenly ask one of her children to go and grab a pen and paper before an idea flies away into the ether.

You can prepare for the random sparks of literary fertility by carrying your phone with you so that you can record voice notes, or dictate an email to yourself that you can later weave into whatever you were writing. It can help to keep a pad of paper and pencil by your bedside too for when you inevitably wake up with an important thought, or even dream about your work. Write it down before it vanishes!

Fitting writing around family life and employment

Given that very few people have the luxury of taking time off to write a book, or having a paid sabbatical in which to write, it is highly likely that you will be fitting your writing around all the other aspects of your life. If you happen to have an understanding family, live-in staff to do the laundry and cooking, a designated writing hut and enough spare cash to do nothing else but write, you can skip this section. If you're still with us we're going to assume that, like us, you might have a paid job, a partner, a house that doesn't seem to have a magic self-cleaning function, toddlers that do not understand the need to stare at a laptop for hours, or teenage angst to navigate.

Is it possible to write while juggling all of life's realities? Why yes of course it is, but you have to be realistic, and kind, to yourself. Here are some of our best hacks for maximising your writing while not opting out of all the rest of it:

- Work out when you might be able to snatch some uninterrupted time to write. Maybe you will get up early and have 2 hours every morning peaceful writing time. As night owls, we're not going to lie to you – this one doesn't appeal to either of us. If you're an early bird and the idea of getting up while everyone else is still asleep and having some peace and quiet sounds sensible, then go for it. Alternatively you might work better in the evenings or late at night. This option can work better for those with younger children as you might have half a chance of them being asleep for a couple of hours after bedtime. Do remember to go to bed yourself though!

- Snatch short periods of time. If your brain allows you to rapidly focus on writing you might find that taking every small opportunity to write can lead to a lot of words being written over time. Don't think that you need really long periods of blocked off time to write. Got 20 minutes whilst dinner is in the oven? Write.

- Multitask and write in different locations. Linked to the point above, this is a particular favourite of Amy's and one she used to write when her children were younger. Children occupied at swimming lessons? Write. Waiting around at school pick up? Write. She even used to take her laptop to meetings so in the ten minutes when everyone was faffing about waiting at the start, she'd write. Sometimes she'd only manage 300 words at once but all those 300 words eventually add up to something much bigger.

- Travel by train instead of driving, and take your laptop. Or persuade someone else to drive if you're travelling together. It's amazing how much you can get done if you have a distinct period of time when you are unlikely to be disturbed by anyone except the conductor checking tickets, and someone periodically walking past offering coffee and snacks.

Getting it done

When it comes to completion, what is a realistic time frame? This is impossible to say, as everyone writes at different speeds. Some people think as they write, and organise their thoughts as they go. Some people have been planning their book in their head for years, so when it comes to writing it, it just pours out. Others sit down and methodically plan out each chapter, with subheadings and sections. Personally, between us, we have used every single approach for different books, but you might find yourself feeling drawn to a particular style.

A separate question from 'how long will it take?', is - 'how will you write your book?'. Most non-fiction books will be somewhere between 50-100k words, which is pretty overwhelming to think about in one go. It can help to develop a strategy in your mind as to how you will tackle this challenge. Some options could be:

One chapter at a time. Some people write their book chronologically, from the beginning to the end, in chapter order. This can makes a lot of sense if you are writing a book that has a clear and logical flow to it, or an argument that needs to be presented in order. Writing the book out of sequence does not always help the book's coherence.

Interest driven writing. Other people start with the chapters they are most interested in because they seem to come out more easily! There's something encouraging about writing a chapter that feels straightforward. You might find that you make rapid progress as you plough through the juiciest parts of your topic. The flip side is that you will be stuck with the harder, more clunky or difficult chapters at the end, but we find that by the time you get to the chapters you're not looking forward to, two things usually have happened. Firstly, you are spurred on by the fact that you have written a large chunk of the book; and secondly, writing large sections before the trickier part often means that the chapter you weren't looking forward to is a little easier because you have made sense of the context.

Chunking it down. Some people subdivide their chapters into small sections, so that it feels less daunting. For example, if you are aiming to write a 60k word book, with 12 chapters of around 5k words each, that still feels like quite a lot of writing. But if you subdivide those chapters into about 10 subheadings, suddenly you are only trying to write a 500-word passage. This is the equivalent of a fairly short blog, and for some people this feels a lot more manageable. This can also be a helpful strategy if you're working on your writing style. Trying to perfect an entire chapter is a big job, but editing and perfecting a 500 word section is more manageable. Writing in chunks can also be a useful way of making sure that you have a cohesive flow to your chapter. Just pay very close attention to the beginnings and ends of those chunks so that they flow logically and seamlessly into the next chunk, avoiding major overlap or repetition.

Word count based goals. Finally, some people set themselves word count targets. We have heard of many PhD students and writers alike who reward themselves with a change in activity, a chocolate bar, or a social media break every thousand words. (You might want to adjust those word counts if you're going for a food-based reward – we take no responsibility for your family coming home to discover you've eaten tonight's dinner.) This sometimes works if you have a definite deadline to work towards. If you wrote 2000 words per day, 5 days per week, you will smash your 60k goal in 6 weeks.

Just a word of warning from someone (Lyndsey) who has tried this particular tactic one or twice.... make sure you are realistic. This includes firstly being reasonable with a daily word count, and secondly, building in a buffer to allow for off days, illness and curve balls. Also, sometimes you will get in the flow and find yourself writing far more - that's fine too. Don't stop because of an arbitrary word count!

Scattergun approach. This is not everyone's cup of tea certainly and may be more suited to those with a solid chunk of writing experience behind them. However, some authors (ahem, Amy) might take what seems like a completely disorganised approach to writing, led by developments that you uncover when reading, or where your thoughts take you. This means that you might start out with a shell for your book and jump from chapter to chapter filling in thoughts and sections as you go. Other people might find this too overwhelming and be at risk of losing days down potential research rabbit holes; but if your brain tends to have multiple thoughts in quickfire succession sometimes just getting them all down and coming back to pad out the gaps later can work well.

Basically, there are many different ways to write. Experiment with finding the approach that feels right to you and lets you feel in as much control as possible with the huge task ahead of you.

Don't force it

One last tip is that if you are truly not in the mood, don't try to write. This includes being stressed or grumpy. It is very hard to write your best work if you are in a bad mood about something. We have both had many times when we have been writing and then something happens to rattle our cages; we have had to either stop and deal with it, whinge to a friend, or make some notes about it before we can be productive again. This is an important thing to do, because otherwise your anger or irritation can be evident in your work. Other days you might simply be too tired. Listen to your body in the same way that you would when you are exercising. Sometimes your brain just needs a break and will be much fresher when you return.

But as well as being tired or in a negative mood, if you are sitting and staring at your desk or laptop and nothing is coming, it's time to step away. Lyndsey has written a lot about sleep, and one of the most basic pieces of advice she ever gives is that the bedtime routine, your bed, and being in bed should be associated with a rapid onset of sleep. If you lie awake worrying, being stressed, or generally struggling to drop off, over time your bed becomes associated with alertness and wakefulness. Not helpful. So the best thing to do if you can't sleep is to get out of your bedroom and do something else.

In the same way, if you're not in a writing mood, don't try to force it. It's helpful for productivity if you associate your writing space with getting work done. If you're messing about, contemplating alphabetizing your books, or rearranging your highlighter pens, this is your cue to go for a walk, watch TV, or talk to a friend. Writing isn't going to happen if you're not feeling it.

And finally, sometimes life just calls for spontaneity. Never feel guilty at taking a break because it's a beautiful sunny day or a friend suggests meeting up. We can all agree that sometimes these things are just good for the soul and in turn the bigger picture progress of your book.

Chapter 8

Overcoming impostor syndrome, perfectionism and other feelings of inadequacy

Although many 'how to write' books focus on the process of improving your writing, we feel that some of the most common barriers to publishing your work are actually psychological. Particularly for female authors and those from under-represented groups; doubts and insecurities can get in the way of starting, finishing and promoting your work - and this is something we want to help you overcome. So if you've ever worried that you're not good enough, or cannot write the perfect piece, then this chapter is for you.

Sometimes it feels as if the world is split into those who have way too much confidence for their actual knowledge and skill, and those who have way too little. As Confucius once said *"Real Knowledge is to know the extent of one's ignorance.'* Yet, sadly, far too many of the first group don't seem to know this, whilst too many of the second group are way too hard about themselves believing they are not qualified, or experienced enough, to share their expertise with others.

We would place a bet that if you've bought this book and are reading this chapter you are probably more likely to fall into the *'don't give myself enough credit'* camp. You hold yourself to high standards, hesitate in releasing your work into the world and just generally worry that you're not good enough to be an author. The good, or bad, news, depending on which way you look at it is that these are such common feelings. We wish we could say that it goes away with the more experience you have and gain, but unfortunately it often seems to work in the other direction. The more you know and the more successful you are, the more you often start to worry about what you might not know.

Although everyone can experience unhelpful feelings like this, they do tend to be more common in women. This is exacerbated by men holding more positions of authority and power and taking up more space and words in public places – or in other words, men have more opportunity to be visible and presented as an expert, shaping our subconscious views on what an expert looks and sounds like. Research has shown that men, particularly those who are older, are viewed by the public as more credible than women and younger people despite their actual experience. This filters through to how young children feel about their abilities and skills, having a knock-on effect on women's confidence from a young age. Couple it with stereotypical views about confident behaviour (e.g. young girls being labelled as bossy rather than assertive or natural leaders) and how women should act (e.g. being kind and supportive of others rather than promoting themselves centre stage) and you have the perfect recipe for impostor syndrome and self-doubt.

Impostor syndrome

Impostor syndrome is the nagging feeling that you simply don't have enough knowledge, skill, or experience to be doing what you're doing - and that everyone else is far more qualified. Sometimes it stops us from taking opportunities in the first place and other times it gives us that continual looking over our shoulder, waiting to be caught out feeling when we're in a role or creating something. It has been described as 'waiting for the tap on the shoulder' – for someone who is a 'real expert' (or 'grown up'?) to come and break the news that everyone has realised that you are nowhere near qualified for your role and would you please now leave.

Dr Valerie Young wrote the brilliant book 'The Secret Thoughts of Successful Women' which focuses on overcoming impostor syndrome, categorising impostor syndrome into five types. These include:

- **The expert** – believes they have to be the best at something in order to do it. If they don't have ALL the knowledge on a topic or are the most knowledgeable, then they shy away. They have a tendency to keep taking courses to improve their skills. They may avoid applying for jobs or roles if they're not highly skilled on all requirements. The expert also finds people complimenting their skills or calling them an expert really uncomfortable.

- **The natural genius** – feels that having to put any effort in to achieve is a sign of failure. These people need to feel that things come naturally and easy to feel successful at something. It doesn't matter if this type *does* achieve greatness, if they didn't do it quickly then it's still a failure. Natural geniuses don't like asking for help or working to improve skills that they're not good at.

- **The perfectionist** – needs everything to be 100% perfect, setting themselves ridiculously high goals and then either failing to meet their own standards, or meeting them and immediately setting new, even higher ones so they never feel successful. Perfectionists struggle to delegate and feel they can always do a better job than anyone else, often leading to overwhelm or burnout.
- **The soloist** – feels that to be successful they have to have achieved everything by themselves. Asking for support or help with an issue equals failure.
- **The superwoman/man** – is convinced they're not as good as everyone else so needs to work ten times harder to simply achieve a basic standard. These people are prone to working very long hours, finding any time off stressful, and are more likely to experience burnout. They may also feel a continual need to prove oneself by achieving new things and rely on others' praise rather than recognising their own success.

Are any (or many) of these ringing a bell? Well, we fully recommend buying Dr Young's book as not only is it full of information about impostor syndrome and overcoming it, but it is just so validating to see it all written down. You can also visit her website to find out lots more https://impostersyndrom.com.

Perfectionism

As mentioned above, perfectionism can be considered a type of impostor syndrome but it is also possible to be a perfectionist without experiencing ongoing impostor syndrome. Perfectionism is the tendency to hold yourself (or indeed others) to impossibly high standards. You continually worry that you are not good enough and could do better. When you do meet the very high standards that you have set for yourself, or achieve something brilliant, you spend a short amount of time feeling proud of yourself before setting yourself new, even higher goals. Whatever goal you just achieved becomes the baseline for minimum performance. You will never get to a place where you are happy enough.

It can be really hard to break out of perfectionism as a core part of the issue is that you believe that if you slow down, don't perform, or indeed fail at something then you will indeed be a complete failure across all aspects of your existence and everyone will lose respect for you. Unsurprisingly perfectionism can therefore go hand in hand with anxiety, depression and low self-esteem.

Wondering whether you're a perfectionist? Well you probably know already if you are or not. Maybe one reason you bought this book is because you're putting off starting, finishing, publishing or promoting your work because you think it's not perfect. However if you are unsure, here are some signs:

- Feeling very upset when criticised
- Obsessing about small details
- Feeling you can't meet others' expectations
- Finding it difficult to make decisions
- Feeling devastated when you have made a mistake
- Worrying about stuff a lot
- Avoiding trying things you might not be good at
- Feeling awful if you miss a deadline or let people down

Central to how you feel might be the fear about whether others think you're a good enough person, which leads you to spend far too much time worrying what others think about you, not complaining about things because you don't want to upset others and finding it difficult to say no. You might also believe that others only like you because of your high standards and achievement and will immediately disown you if you relax or falter a bit.

You might also have a tendency to hold others to your own high standards and end up feeling continually let down when they don't overachieve too. Maybe you find it impossible to delegate tasks, find it difficult to trust other people to complete work or get irritated when people don't do things well.

Overcoming feelings of inadequacy and perfectionism

The important question of course is how do we overcome these feelings of being caught out / not being good enough / needing to be perfect all the time? It's not easy and involves challenging your own thinking and behaviour, but there are strategies to help you feel more relaxed and confident over time.

1. Recognise what you do know

One way to challenge your tendency to perfectionism or impostor syndrome is to tackle that belief that you don't have enough experience. Challenge that nagging voice in your brain. The one that says you don't know enough / other people know more / you are wrong about everything. It is highly unlikely that this voice is accurate, although recognising what you don't know and changing your mind when you find new evidence is of course a brilliant skill. Don't ever completely stop challenging yourself. However, if you can find some balance between self-doubt and self-worth this would be fabulous.

One way to overcome this and reassure yourself is by making a list of all the different experiences that have led you to this point. You can do this at any time but it can be a particularly good exercise around milestones – birthdays, New Year, anniversaries and indeed book launches. This list will differ according to your background and the aim of your book, but could include:

- Qualifications and training
- Experience in supporting others, for example as a professional or volunteer
- Conducting research
- Previous writing such as blogs or research articles
- Social media pages and reach
- Niche interests such as having read a lot around a topic
- Your own lived experience such as a health issue or charity work
- Awards and successes including making a difference to others

All of these have likely honed your knowledge and expertise, but they are more than the sum of their parts. Different elements of your experience have weaved together, alongside considerable time and effort, to create your expertise. They have enabled you to have a 'big picture view' of a topic. You understand how pieces of evidence and experiences fit together. You know the methodology and limitations of research papers compared to the media headlines that are shared. You understand the small signs that indicate that a complication in a situation you are supporting is serious.

Have you ever seen one of those iceberg diagrams, used perhaps to illustrate a behaviour such as success in sport? The concept is that what you see on the surface is only a tiny bit of someone's expertise. So you see someone scoring goals, but you don't see the hours of training, fitness programmes and specialist diets that got them there. This leads to the (incorrect) self-belief amongst some that they could play just as well in a premier league game if they had the opportunity. Of course they couldn't, but that doesn't stop them believing it, and for a long time as they never get the opportunity to be proven wrong.

Why is this like writing? Well it's about recognising the strengths and experiences that you have as a writer in terms of whatever brought you to write this book. It's about acknowledging that to yourself, having confidence in it and drawing upon it to write your book. Keep going back to that list of skills above. You have the evidence of your experience, now believe in it.

2. Experiment with your behaviour

If you are feeling overwhelmed with the pressure of achieving and being perfect it can help to slowly wean yourself off this need. You are the one most likely driving your expectations. What would happen if you reduced the pressure you put on yourself? Would your progress irreparably slow down? Would your reputation disappear? We bet not, but you need to take the first step in tentatively experimenting with your comfort point.

Make a list of your non-negotiables when it comes to your standards and a list of things that probably do not matter. Maybe this is in terms of how much you achieve. Will it hurt to perform a little less often? Do you really need to write that blog / spend that time on social media / do that presentation? What would it mean if you were still productive but didn't do all the things? Try saying no when people ask you to do things. Start small. How does it feel? What could you do with the saved time? One trick Amy (a self-confessed over-worker) uses is to make an 'I said no' list with tasks she says no to, and estimated time saved. It adds up to an eye-opening amount of time which could be used in better ways (including sitting doing nothing).

If you struggle with starting or finishing work because you think it has to be perfect, then try just getting on with it! This might sound simple and infuriating at the same time but what would happen if you just started a document and made notes, wrote a 'good enough' draft before moving onto the next chapter, or sent something off to your editor that wasn't entirely polished? How much perfectly imperfect progress would you make compared to doing, well... nothing?

Another idea is to experiment with the reaction you receive if you do something that isn't 100% perfect by your standards. Try putting something out into the world that isn't perfect. Start with something small that doesn't really matter, such as a blog on something interesting but not controversial. You could set yourself a time limit to write it, meaning you don't spend hours poring over it. Write it, check it over, get it out there. What happens? Is the world still turning?

3. Think about why you might feel this way

Another approach is to try and give yourself time and space to think about why you might feel this way. Why are you feeling so much pressure or doubt? What are you afraid of and why? Who told you that you weren't good enough? Who are you trying to prove things to? Or who told you that you were only good enough if you were overachieving? Understanding why you feel this way helps you stop and think about how you could move forward. You might be able to do this alone. One technique to help you process these thoughts is to do something active such as swimming, or a long walk, that distracts your body physically so that you can think. Or you might benefit from some coaching or counselling to get to the root of the issue.

You could also try challenging any negative thoughts, reminding yourself that they are incorrect and you have evidence of this. Some psychologists suggest even personifying your thoughts, making them into a funny or pitiful character. Now when you find yourself thinking perfectionist thoughts, imagine it in a squeaky or daft voice. Surely you can't take orders from that?

4. Ask some trusted friends for feedback

If you are worried about your level of productivity or achievement, talk to some friends whom you trust. This could be in terms of constructive feedback on your work and strengths, or it could be a bigger picture conversation about how we all spend time faffing about, getting distracted by other tasks and feeling inadequate or unmotivated at times. Just because you weren't productive this week, or had challenging thoughts, this doesn't mean you are abnormal or something is wrong with you. Quite the opposite in fact!

It can help to have a circle of writing friends (or join a group on social media) that help you keep things in perspective. Some open and honest conversations about how long things can take or how much time other people spend procrastinating can put things in perspective. You might like to check our website **www.thoughtrebellion.com** for our upcoming writing support groups and workshops.

Chapter 17 - Dealing with criticism is also pertinent here, in particular thinking about whose opinion you are going to trust and whose you will ignore. Although it is important to remain humble and open to constructive feedback, you cannot let everyone's attempts to criticise you and bring you down distract you.

5. Show yourself the same kindness (and respect) you would a friend

We are often our own worst enemies when it comes to judging ourselves. Imagine you are a friend. What do you think of 'their' achievements and skills? Do you think they are useless and not performing? Inadequate? What would you say to them if they were feeling like you were?

Don't compare yourself directly to friends and other colleagues, particularly if you don't really know much about their working or home lives. Maybe they have a job that fits with their writing more seamlessly. Maybe their children are older. Maybe they have a partner who is really supportive, or indeed away a lot so they use writing to distract themselves. There are so many different factors in our lives that can impact upon our productivity (perceived or otherwise). Remember we have a tendency to only show our best bits on things like social media. We play down how much effort it took us and our mistakes and only showcase our successes.

It can help to recognise all the other things that you have going on too. If you feel that you're not achieving or writing fast enough then make a list of all your responsibilities. Maybe you have a job or other commitments, children or caring responsibilities, or a health condition. Recognise what you are achieving as opposed to what you are not, or what you are achieving in spite of everything else you have going on.

6. Recognise how self-styled experts can exacerbate your feelings

Linked to the previous point about not comparing yourself to others is the importance of recognising the difference between those who have spent time building their expertise and those who just have a very strong belief in themselves. Just because someone has published a book / is very vocal on social media / shouts a lot about how great they are ... doesn't mean they actually have any real expertise.

Indeed, while some of us might be battling the impostor syndrome and perfectionist demons, at the opposite end of the scale are the self-styled experts who could do with a dose of self-doubt. People in this category tend to overestimate how much they know and are typically not shy to a) shout about how much of an expert they are and b) criticise others (who often have more knowledge than they do). The primary issue with this confidence is that these people often don't realise how much they don't know.

Unfortunately people are quick to criticise experts based on what they don't know. This might be in relation to not realising the depth of an expert's knowledge or an underestimation of how much learning and experience has gone on to make someone an expert. People who feel like this tend to overestimate their abilities based on very little experience, and fail to see all the effort that others put in. A good example of this is the finding by YouGov that one in eight men believe they could score a point off Serena Williams in a tennis match (compared to one in 33 women)[4]. Presumably those who felt they could do this take their experience of being quite good at tennis amongst their mates and somehow believe that matches the effort that Serena puts in. They fail to see the many hours of practice, specialist diet, coaching, etc that she puts in (and that's before we throw in genetics and natural talent).

This is captured in the Dunning - Kruger phenomenon which refers to an unfortunately strong correlation that often the less competent and knowledgeable someone is, the stronger their belief that they are somehow extremely informed, whilst simultaneously believing those who are viewed as experts in the area have much poorer abilities. You see this play out all the time on social media with people who have little experience or awareness criticising those who have far more.

Unfortunately, self-styled experts have the impact of making much more qualified people start to doubt themselves. Don't let them. See points 1 – 5 and focus on building your own work.

---

[4] YouGov (2019) Could you win a point off Serena Williams? https://bit.ly/3NuVR48

Chapter 9

Honing your writing skills

It's likely that if you're planning to write a book then you have some basic experience of writing for others. This might be as simple as writing blogs or social media posts, or maybe you have more professional experience of writing in a work capacity. Maybe you're reading this with a book or two already under your belt with the aim of developing your skills and growing as a writer.

We believe that writing is a skill that keeps growing alongside you. There is always room to hone your skills and become a better writer, no matter what your experience. While this may feel daunting, it means that the quality of your work in years to come may be even better than it is now. Most authors look back on their first book, and think of a hundred ways to make it better. Whether you are a first-time writer or you're contemplating your 10th book, the truth is that there is always room for improvement (and this goes for us too!).

There are many ways to get better at writing and entire books are devoted to this subject. For now here are our top tips that have helped us develop our work:

1. **Read more books, journals, articles and anything you can get your hands on**

Reading as much as you can, of a variety of books as you can, is a wonderful way to build your writing skill. This is for three main reasons:

- It increases your knowledge of a subject
- It exposes you to many different types of writing
- It opens your mind to different styles and provides inspiration

One of the things we have learnt over and over is that explaining a complex concept simply comes from a deep understanding of the subject. You will be a better teacher through your writing when you are well-versed in not only your subject, but from reading around your subject and understanding any counter argument.

Secondly, reading more will help you to be passively exposed to a vast variety of different types and styles of writing. You will not be able to avoid being affected by this. We recommend reading authors from different eras, genres, cultures and styles. It will expand your vocabulary and help you learn how to phrase sentences with more finesse.

You should read widely. Read classical literature, modern trashy beach fodder, Sunday Times bestsellers, quirky books, journal articles – everything you can get your hands on. You won't like everything you read, and that's ok too. But the simple process of choosing books – both fiction and non-fiction, reading them and deciding what you like and don't like will mean you pick up and filter ideas.

2. Developing critical thinking skills

The next part about all that reading we're recommending, is to really think about what you're reading. Do you like it? If so, why? Why don't you like it? Why have you underlined that paragraph? What is it that makes that sentence so perfect? How has the author managed to render you speechless?

Think about the quotes that are so good you want to frame them and also think about what you don't like. Why don't you like that passage, chapter, or entire book? Did it not grab your attention? Was it inaccurate? Ridiculous? Unhelpful? Hard-going? Was it poorly written? If so, be specific about what you thought the errors were.

Critical thinking is especially important when you are reading journals and articles or researching different perspectives for your own book. How do you develop critical thinking skills? Well, there are lots of ways you might have heard of – some are specific to certain fields or situations. We suggest:

Acknowledging your own assumptions, beliefs and biases. This means owning that you do have these and accepting that these beliefs might influence your perceptions and ability to be open minded. Start with what you think you believe about the topic you are reading about. Write down your assumptions if you like. Nobody else needs to know the details but it's important to be honest with yourself.

To test your own unconscious bias try the Project Implicit website run by Harvard University - it has numerous tests for various biases and can help you identify areas where you may need to be more aware: https://implicit.harvard.edu/implicit/takeatest.html.

Don't believe everything you read. Challenge what the author has written by questioning whether it is logical, reasonable, valid or sensible. Look for how the author has backed up what they are saying. Have they provided any evidence? Do the numbers add up? Do you understand what their study was about? If you don't, (there's no shame in that by the way) you cannot possibly critique or use the study if you do not understand the methodology or how they came by their results.

Present a counter argument to what the author has written. Play devil's advocate! Do you remember being on debating teams in high school? Were you ever on a side you didn't actually feel aligned with but went through the process as an academic / learning exercise? That is what this is all about. Whether your inclination is to look for reasons to agree with or to refute the study you are reading, practice the discipline of getting on the other side and challenging those assumptions you hold.

In some cases, to properly critique something you may have to read up on the subject. We saw a tweet recently that basically pointed out that research was spending all day reading 30 papers so that you can reference one paper in one sentence. This is exactly what we mean. Sometimes to understand one paper, you need to read around that paper to get a balanced view. You just need to accept this if you are committed to producing evidence-based work.

Learn to spot waffle, jargon and filler. There is a big difference between writing that requires many words to help the reader make sense of something, or writing that helps the author form a rapport with the reader, and wordiness or fluff. Sometimes papers have paragraphs that could be summarised in one short sentence. Learn to look out for this, as the writing might look clever on the face of it but there isn't much substance. This should put you on alert for other.

Ask 'why' a lot as you read something. Why did you do that? Why did you think that? Why did you form that conclusion? Why did you choose that sample? Why didn't you have a bigger and more diverse sample? Why did you choose that method? As you ask these 'why' questions, see if the writing answers them. If *you* are asking the question, the author should have asked themselves that question too and should be able to provide justification.

Practice thinking about the counter argument. 'Couldn't that finding be explained by x?' Basically, be the annoying student at the back of the class trying to be a smartass. Don't worry, nobody will know!

3. **Learn how to improve your sentence structure, language and use of literary devices.**

Fundamentally, improving your writing means learning how to make each sentence count. This means not only the avoidance of writing errors (we'll get to those), but also thinking about how you write on a micro-level. When we are considering our book, we often leap to the macro – the chapters and overall book purpose. This is obviously important, but the micro-level structuring of each sentence is what will elevate your work. As you develop the process of carefully choosing your words and using more interesting language on a frequent basis this will begin to feel more intuitive, we promise!

Literary devices are language tools that writers use to convey their meaning. You probably use some of them already, even if the only reason you are familiar with them is because you've helped your child with their English homework. Some of them, such as alliteration, are much less relevant for non-fiction writing but here are a few you could consider using in your work, if and when they are appropriate.

Metaphor and simile: These are a comparison of two unrelated things. A simile is almost the same as a metaphor except that it uses the word 'like'. Saying 'Writing a book is a beast' is a metaphor, whereas saying 'Writing a book is like a beast' is a simile. Metaphors and similes can help readers understand your meaning better, particularly if the subject matter is novel to them because it makes a comparison with something that is more well-known.

Alliteration: This is the practice of using words with the same starting letter in consecutive words in a short phrase or sentence for emphasis. As mentioned, it's less relevant in general for non-fiction writing. Children learning about alliteration in creative writing often come up with sentences such as 'the wet, wild, windy wood'. This can certainly have its place. It's not very useful if you're trying to make a serious point, as it can sound forced. However, occasionally alliteration can make something really memorable. For instance, Lyndsey coined the term 'wonky winding' some years ago to describe the practice of laying a baby on their left side to facilitate digestion and easy winding. It went viral because it's catchy, despite there being nothing particularly innovative about the practice and regardless of the fact that many people have used the technique for decades.

Analogy: In many ways analogy is also similar to metaphors and similes because analogy is about once again making a comparison to aid understanding. However, with an analogy the two unrelated things often have some similar features. For example, if someone was explaining how children learn, they might say that forming synaptic connections in the brain is a little like laying a path. Over time, as that path gets more well-used or has more traffic, we might expand the path or even make a road. The road makes it even quicker to get people where they need to be. In the same way, the more we practise something, the more the synapse becomes myelinated, allowing messages in the brain to be transmitted rapidly. Analogies really help a reader to make sense of a new concept.

Acronym: Acronyms are words formed from the first letter of several words in a phrase. Almost everyone uses acronyms in their everyday speech - for instance; ASAP (As Soon As Possible), ETA (Estimated Time of Arrival), TBC (To be Confirmed). Sometimes people create a phrase with a memorable acronym in mind. While this can sometimes sound forced, it can help people to remember. For example, researchers sometimes use acronyms to make their study more catchy - like the CHILD study, which is a large project that continues to generate data. CHILD stands for Canadian Healthy Infant Longitudinal Development - clearly the acronym rolls off the tongue far more easily and this helps with dissemination of study findings.

Hyperbole: This is a gross exaggeration that drives a point home. For example, if someone was describing the mental load of parenting toddlers, they might say something like 'when you are at home and your 3-year-old has asked you eleven million times for a chocolate bar'. The use of hyperbole in this example makes it clearer that this kind of situation is fatiguing and frustrating much more than if they'd simply said; 'when you are at home and your 3-year-old asks repeatedly for a chocolate bar'. The second example, while more factually accurate, does not depict the emotional burden of the scenario as well as the first. By contrast, exaggeration is just language that is over the top and might not even be interpreted as exaggeration by everyone. For example, you might describe a bad day as a 'disaster' if you were exaggerating, but you might describe it as apocalyptic using hyperbole. You might claim that your stubbed toe is 'killing you' if you were using hyperbole, but say that it was 'agony' if you were exaggerating. Hyperbole is an extreme or unrealistic exaggeration and there should be no way anyone would think you are being literal.

Imagery: This is the use of descriptive language that helps a reader to imagine a scene. For example, if someone was trying to describe how stress feels, using imagery would be an effective literary device. They might describe the fluttering in someone's stomach, the sinking feeling of doom, the anxious racing thoughts, the sweaty palms, rapid heart rate and feeling of nausea, as well as the heightened sense of awareness and alertness – taking in the sights, sounds and smells around them if they are feeling stressed. Painting a vivid picture of a scene helps the reader to position themselves in that moment and understand the context.

Personification: This is when we ascribe human characteristics to animals or objects. For example, if we were trying to convey some of the feelings and mental load of being a writer, we might say, 'The laptop sits conspicuously in the corner of the room, silently chastising me for wilfully ignoring it all day.' Using personification can say something about underlying feelings. It can also make an everyday object more meaningful, or a seemingly innocuous experience more profound and relatable. Some more academic journals and texts frown on phrases that use personification inappropriately; for example 'this study found that...', this is personification because of course the study itself didn't find anything. The researcher was the one who found out whatever it was, so it is technically not an accurate use of language. Basically, a writing style may be helpful in some contexts and disapproved of in others - it's all about knowing your audience.

Onomatopoeia: This is using a word that when said aloud, makes the sound you're describing. Typical examples include 'click', 'whoosh', 'drip', clunk' and so on. Occasionally, using onomatopoeic words can add richness especially when you think about how your book might sound if it was narrated. Using it too much can give your work a childlike quality so be careful with this one, only using it when it adds something to the description in your writing.

There are two main cautions we have with literary devices. The first is that as with any tool if you overuse it, it can become stale, repetitive or irritating. The second is to be aware of your audience. Not all these literary devices are appropriate for every audience - some are best chosen for an academic audience, while others work better for an accessible book aimed at a non-academic readership. Some people find literary devices difficult to understand if their interpretation of language is literal, or are reading in a second or more language.

For example, some figurative language, such as hyperbole, irony and metaphor can be more difficult for some people to decode, making accessibility a problem. Many people, for example neurodiverse readers, who may interpret language literally *are* able to decode figurative language, but it can make their job harder, so consider how much of it you should use with your audience in mind. The same applies if you think your work may be read by readers of another language – figurative language does not always translate well, as anyone who has ever tried using Google translate knows!

4. Practice telling stories.

All writers are storytellers at heart. If you can tell a good everyday story, you're on the road to becoming a good writer. Nobody enjoys a boring story - in fact, this is a great example of an oxymoron. Your writing should engage your reader. You can do this in a number of ways – using humour, varying your language, using literary devices and making sure your writing avoids either overly superfluous description, or short clipped sentences without any expansion. Judicious use of irony, humour and anecdote can bring your author's voice to life but this should not be used at the expense of making your book useful.

Another important part of storytelling is to speak to your readers and tell them why this subject matters to them. People want to connect with an author and the subject they are talking about. They want to see themselves in the examples you are giving. For some subjects this is really easy. If you are writing about parenting, health or any topic that has humans at its heart, then connecting to people with examples from everyday life is relatively simple. The data and evidence you use will be based on people. But if your topic is natural science or engineering this might be trickier. Include all the technical information about your data, but also link it back to people, everyday language and what it means for the person reading your book.

We stress this point elsewhere, but don't get caught up in thinking that you have to be deadly serious and use big words in order to be considered an expert. Readability and connection is so important in engaging with your reader and encouraging them to keep on reading. If something is written in a dry and mind-numbing style, it doesn't matter how important or accurate it is, your reader will have to be pretty committed to keep on going. Likewise don't think that you have to use highly scientific language to appear expert. Sometimes simple descriptions are far better because they allow your readers to understand and not feel excluded or out of place because they don't know the technical jargon. If you do need to use scientific or technical terms, explain what they mean. And it goes without saying that you should never include a term or word that you don't understand.

5. Listen to criticism of your work with humility and allow this to shape your writing.

Although this tip might feel scarily intimidating, ask people whose work you respect for their opinion and listen with humility. If there is someone you admire, or who knows about your subject, you would be wise to listen openly to any and all advice they have to offer. This does not mean they are right. It's a well-known fact that clever people are sometimes just plain wrong. But you should apply those critical thinking skills and sift their advice. This starts with humility, and acknowledging that none of us is a perfect writer or has written the perfect book. Be willing to accept honest feedback and you will grow enormously as a writer. Listening and learning from criticism is a hard but important part of growing as a writer - you might want to read more about this in the section on how to handle criticism (Chapter 17).

6. Learn how to avoid writing pitfalls

We'll readily admit that this is a challenging section to write because we (like everyone else) are not perfect writers. We are also not expert editors and you may well accuse us of breaking our own rules sometimes in places! You can undertake entire degree programmes on English and Creative Writing and probably still feel like you could know more about the rules of writing. Sometimes rules are made to be broken and this goes for writing too, but it's important to have an understanding of writing etiquette in the first place to know when you can break those rules. Here are just a few major writing pitfalls you should try to avoid:

Spelling, punctuation and grammar: We have all read books that have spelling, grammatical or punctuation mistakes. Spotting spelling mistakes and typos are really hard when you are immersed in your work and even more so if you have an additional challenge such as dyslexia or dyspraxia, or are neurodiverse. Word processing software can help but it doesn't always catch errors such as writing 'from' instead of 'form'. Unfortunately these errors can end up changing the entire meaning of the sentence, or render it incomprehensible.

Other times, we use a word accidentally. Lyndsey once used 'months' when she meant 'years' and this was not picked up by either the spell check, two edits or the proofreader. It was only picked up by a hawk-eyed reader after publication. These small errors from time to time are fairly inevitable but try to read your work closely. Some people find it is easier to spot typos and grammatical problems when reading passages out of sequence, so you're not distracted by the content flow but are able to focus on the language.

If you have an editor and proofreader as part of your publishing package this will go some way to helping pick up these errors, although they may not spot all technical ones. If you are self-publishing and can afford it, proofreading is a good investment, even if it's a budget option of swapping favours with a skilled friend. We have more tips on this in 'Editing your work' in Chapter 12.

Wrong balance of explanation or description: This is where too much or too little description or explanation is used. Remember, if you're writing a reference book, long flowery descriptions may not be welcome. Unlike fiction, your reader does not need to immerse themselves in your description. Long waffly paragraphs without much theoretical content, action point or practical take-home message are frustrating and leave most readers silently pleading 'get to the point'.

On the other hand, too little description can make your writing feel cold and clinical, and you may also struggle to meet your word count. This is obviously fine if you're writing a clinical textbook, but assuming you are not, you will need to provide your reader with the right amount of background. This balance is very hard to get right and this is where having some honest feedback is invaluable. You need enough description to engage your reader and be personable, without descending into pages and pages of wordiness.

Inadequate handling of controversy: If your work includes a difficult, sensitive, divisive or controversial topic, then you will need to be careful about how you handle this. Be especially careful if you have no personal experience as your writing may come across as lacking credibility or authenticity. With difficult or controversial topics it is *especially* important to be factually accurate, as failure to get the basics right may be a source of pain, distress or anger for your reader; as well as being an area for negative critique about your writing. Make sure you are fastidious in your sentence structure as people who are sensitive to a topic will read negativity into it. For example, being cautious by adding in a few 'might' or 'could' and acknowledging how others may have different views or experiences can go a long way.

Another pitfall to avoid is being too generic in your description of the controversial topic, as this can seem like you are paying 'lip-service' to it which can feel insensitive. Finally, acknowledge your bias and be compassionate towards those who may well have an opposing view or feel excluded by anything inflammatory. Both of us write about two of the most controversial topics in the early parenting world – breastfeeding and sleep, we've learned from experience that you have to handle these topics with delicacy!

Too much personal opinion: Of course we bring our own views and experiences to our work, but be cautious about oversharing. Relying on personal opinion or experience can feel nauseating to a reader. Sometimes self-reflection is appropriate, and in a memoir it is the driving style. However, in general try to avoid overuse of this as it will feel irrelevant to many of your readers. It is also a potential source of criticism of your work if you have not backed up your writing with published sources, but relied on experience or anecdote. It is natural that as you write, some personal feelings and thoughts will bubble to the surface because writing is often cathartic. One way to get around these thoughts infiltrating your work too much is to offload your personal thoughts or experiences in a journal or separate file.

Lack of logical flow: As we have alluded to a few times, your writing needs to guide your reader through a thought process that is logical. Hopping around, repeating ideas and illogical trains of thought are nightmarish for a reader. Your work should have a clear beginning, middle and end, as well as intermediary chapters. Beyond that, each chapter either needs to act as a conduit to the next, or be distinctly different, while still flowing well. This does not mean that you have to write the book in this order, but do pay attention to the flow of your book as you go. The best way to tell if your work flows logically is to ask someone without knowledge of the subject to read it and provide honest feedback. It might feel tempting to leave this until the editing stage, but this is really too late, as major restructuring may alter the flow and feel of the whole book.

Wordiness: This is frustrating to a reader who cannot find the point you're trying to make due to unnecessary words. All of us can be prone to this, but be especially careful when you have written a skeleton outline but find your word count is coming up short. What you should never do at this point is pad your sentences out with fluff. Elaborate paragraphs or endless pages of text with no subheadings or paragraph breaks can be off putting. It's daunting just to look at, but once you start reading it is even worse. A classic way that we introduce wordiness is by using three or four words when one would work. 'In certain situations, such as…', can be more simply written as 'when'. 'Owing to the fact that' can more simply be written as 'because'. As you critically proofread your work ask yourself how often you drift towards wordiness.

Incorrect or inappropriate use of conjunctions: This is a controversial point. We in no way wish to sound like the grammar police or suggest that there is one 'right' way of writing, but some writing styles may attract criticism. Some people consider 'incorrect' use of conjunctions to be a grammatical error while others would barely notice, or even appreciate them. This includes starting sentences with 'And', and 'But'. The mnemonic FANBOYS is a reminder of the main conjunctions 'for', 'and', 'nor', 'but', 'or', 'yet', 'so'. Not everyone agrees with this so it is another example of how you need to know your target audience.

Use of conjunctions at the start of sentences can work well in less formal writing or when skilfully used to add emphasis, but this depends on what you are writing and who you are writing for. It is rarely acceptable to start a sentence with a conjunction in academic writing for example, but for many other audiences it may be appropriate and help bring your words to life. Avoiding starting a sentence with 'and', or 'but' can be hard because many authors write in the same way that they speak. You can absolutely get away with this style of writing if you are writing for wide appeal, but it helps to at least understand why some people prefer to abide by this rule before you know when it is acceptable to judiciously break it. The reason against starting sentences with a conjunction is that it can make a paragraph feel like an endless string of slightly related thoughts. We'll offer an example:

> *So, let's say you have written a book which you'd love the world to read. And this book is your life's work, full to the brim with useful information that will create impact. And you'd like the book to be a respected resource in your field. But you also want the book to be accessible and readable by a large audience. So you decide that you will avoid endless strings of sentences that are full of clauses or clarification. And this means that you'll need to re-write this entire paragraph because it sounds like a twelve-year-old has had a five minute stream of consciousness!*

By contrast, this is the same information but without using conjunctions at the start of the sentences:

> *You've written a book which you'd love the world to read, based on your life's work. The book is full to the brim with useful information that will create impact, deserving of being a respected resource in your field. In order to make the book accessible and readable by a large audience, you have chosen to avoid endless strings of sentences that start with clauses.*

By rewriting this paragraph you have successfully conveyed the same message but with more maturity (and you've cut the word count down as well). If you're unsure about how and when to break this rule or whether you're using conjunctions too much, your editor will be able to help you, but if you are self-publishing you will save a lot of time and money to carefully scrutinise your work for overuse of this style before you send your first draft.

Over-emphasis: This is where additional expletives are used, for example saying; 'It is *incredibly* important' or 'it is *absolutely* essential'. Not only does this contribute to wordiness but it can also be disingenuous. Is it really *that* important or essential? Sometimes an expletive can be used appropriately, so we don't mean that they are *always* poor writing practice (see what we did there?). Comb through your work and check for over-emphasis as it can make writing irritating to read. This particular pitfall also makes your word look less academically credible as it is hard to justify why something is 'very' or 'really' important. On a related note, be careful about being too decisive unless something is certain. Saying one factor 'may' lead to something else is safer than saying it 'will'.

Another way that over-emphasis can be avoided is by checking for too many exclamation marks. When you add exclamation marks frequently it can make your writing seem over-enthusiastic, like the literary equivalent of an excited, tail-wagging Labrador puppy. Exclamation marks add excitement! They can add drama! They add suspense! When we see them in text, we are supposed to react and this can be powerful. When we overuse them, however, the effect can be faintly exhausting.

7. Being inspired by mentors

Finally, you will learn a great deal by attending conferences, reading books and papers and talking to authors or researchers whose work you respect. Not only will they educate you on your subject material but they may help you to think about areas you hadn't considered. You will also find it inspiring. Whilst you should not try to emulate their writing style – after all, it should be your voice that comes through your writing – you can be inspired by the way they present. More experienced writers or speakers may have a unique style but they also have learned many of the skills in this chapter, and immersing yourself in good quality writing is a great way to learn how to be even better at what you love.

Chapter 10

How to understand and use evidence

Backing up your writing with evidence is a central part of crafting many non-fiction books. Although your practical and lived experience can play a really important role, when it comes to talking about the bigger picture, making sure your statements are as evidence based as possible is vital. It's important to share accurate information with your readers but it also means that your critics have less ground to challenge your work as it is backed up by evidence. Being research led and balanced is a big part of being taken seriously as an non-fiction author.

This section therefore looks at good sources of information, where to find evidence, and how to understand research. If you write for a living in other ways, are a researcher, or perhaps are used to writing reports for work then you might already be aware of what is included in this section – that said, it has some useful book recommendations if you want to take things further. If it has been a while since you studied, or you took a different route to where you are now, then this section should give you some good ideas of where to start.

What types of research and evidence should I cite?

When you are using evidence to support your writing, there are many different sources you can use. What you choose will depend on the context and content of what you are writing. There are no outright 'bad' sources of information, but some do have more limitations than others. Some useful data sources include:

Journal articles: If you are looking for evidence to support a 'fact' (such as a certain diet being associated with a certain health outcome) then it is best to use a journal article. Journal articles report directly on research that has been conducted. They are then reviewed by other academics for quality and accuracy, usually going through a series of revisions to improve the paper. They contain all the details of what you need to judge whether the findings are useful or not such as the methods used and sample size.

Policy documents: These are great for citing recommendations such as health recommendations or housing policy. It's good practice if you read any useful studies in a policy document or other report to go and read the research paper, rather than just copying what the report has said. They might have reported it inaccurately and it's important to see the bigger picture of what the research did (and did not) do.

Statistical documents and reports: Sources such as the Office for National Statistics often publish useful reports on rates of things occurring. For example, birth rate and death rate, housing, crime figures and so on. Other public organisations such as public health bodies may collect statistics relevant to your topic.

Charity reports: Charities and other organisations may conduct research into a topic. It is more likely to have limitations in terms of who took part and how well the research was reviewed but can be particularly useful for qualitative data and lived experiences.

You *can* also cite other sources including blogs, news articles and websites but it's important to state the limitations and relevance of the information. For example, you might write that 'In an eye-opening documentary the BBC explored...' but you wouldn't cite the BBC as having conducted research. You might cite an interesting blog that talks about the challenges some parents face in keeping their child active, but you wouldn't use it to support a statement that 'child physical activity supports social development'. For that you would be better placed to use journal articles.

If a media source refers to a research study it's really important to go to the source of the research and read it yourself firstly to get a fuller picture of the study but also because media headlines often have the tendency to be sensational or weighted towards one line of argument. They are not reliable sources of 'facts' but can be useful sources of 'interesting occurrences'.

How to find evidence

It's best to do a structured search for the evidence to go in your book. You could simply use Google, but doing this will get you every last article or story on the topic. The best approach is to use a journal search engine.

These can differ by your subject area but some of the most common ones to use are:

- Google scholar https://scholar.google.co.uk
- PubMed https://pubmed.ncbi.nlm.nih.gov
- Web of science https://wok.mimas.ac.uk
- Medline https://www.medline.com
- Social Science Research Network (SSRN) https://www.ssrn.com

Google scholar is a firm favourite here as it is simple to use. You can refine your search limits by date to keep your search relevant. It also lets you know whether you can freely access the full text. Google scholar also shows you how many times a paper has been cited by other papers. This is a measure of popularity of the paper but isn't necessarily an indicator of quality. After all, other researchers could be including that paper as an example of what not to do!

Using key search words

You only get out of a search engine what you put in. So think about the words that you use. It's good practice to make a list. Include all similar words and phrases, regional / country variations and spellings. You can also use set words known as Boolean operators in most search engines to limit or broaden your search. Quite simply these let you search for multiple words or exclude certain words. This is useful if search terms for your topic cross over into other areas. For example, Amy does research on babies starting solid foods, which parents often refer to as 'weaning'. She learnt long ago not to simply search for 'weaning' as you get a load of papers about weaning pigs and weaning patients off ventilators.

AND – to search for things that have two specific characteristics e.g. Babies AND Flu
OR – to search broadly for one or more topics that are different to each other e.g. Pregnancy OR childbirth
NOT – to exclude things e.g. weaning NOT pigs

What if I can't access the paper I want?

The world of academic publishing is very strange. Unlike book publishing where the author receives royalties for publishing a book, when researchers get a research paper accepted it is often hidden behind a paywall. To access it you either have to be part of an institution that subscribes to that journal such as a university of health organisation or pay to download an article. This is where the strange bit comes into play – the researchers i.e. the authors don't receive any of that money. Even stranger, if the authors want the option of everyone being able to access it for free, they can do so if they (usually their university of research grant) pays thousands of pounds. This means that research you can freely access is often skewed towards the big topics that get lots of research funding such as cancer and heart disease rather than chronic illness or women's health.

However, there is a perfectly legal loophole. Researchers are allowed to send out copies of their papers to individuals. Their email is usually on the paper (look for 'corresponding author' or if you can't see that, Google them) and you can contact them and ask for a copy. You might be able to find a preprint online too. A preprint is the author's copy of a paper pre-publication. It might be the version before peer review or the version before it gets typeset by the journal (the journal controls which version they are allowed to self-archive i.e. make available). However, do bear in mind that the paper might change after review, so if you are citing it rather than just reading it, it's best to ask the author for a copy.

Avoiding cherry picking

Ideally when you are researching a book you ought to start by conducting a thorough review of all the literature to examine what the overall pattern of evidence is for your topic. You would read lots of different studies and then sit down to begin writing your book. Nevertheless, in reality we know it doesn't always happen this way. Although this version might reflect the timeline of an academic writer who is immersed in the literature for their subject; you might have had your idea for your book many years into a professional career, or after years of volunteering or other relevant experiences. You have witnessed something frequently happening (or not happening) in your day to day practice and spot a gap for a book.

The temptation at this point is to write down everything you know and then do a literature review in reverse where you scan the literature to find a study to support your point. You search through Google until you find a study, maybe even ignoring other studies that don't support what you are saying. By doing this you have indeed provided evidence to back up your point, although it is quite possible that you are missing (or ignoring) other studies that contradict what you are stating. Unless you then also go and perform a wider review of other papers on the topic in order to understand the bigger picture, you are doing something known as 'cherry-picking'.

Cherry picking is something we all have a tendency to do because it feels great to find studies that support what we are passionate about, or have experienced in our practice or lives. Be aware that all studies have limitations to them and will have been conducted using different methods and perspectives; it really is important to look at the bigger picture and think about what other similar studies are showing. No one study is ever meant to provide the full picture of evidence on a topic. It is meant to contribute to the overall jigsaw of data on a subject and then this combination of studies is used to draw conclusions. Therefore, to perform a thorough review of the literature you need to read multiple papers. What is the trend in the data when you look at them? Why might they find different things? What are the strengths or limitations in studies that differ to other similar ones?

This doesn't mean that you can't use interesting studies that are showing something different to the rest. However, this is where it is important to make this transparent in your language. You can use phrases such as 'one study found that' to make it clear that it was just one study. Or you could point out how the study you are using was conducted differently to the others and that is why it has different findings. So, you could write 'Although many studies find that X is unrelated to Y, one study that measured X in a different and more rigorous way found...'. You could also highlight how other studies have important limitations such as the sample size used, date of the research or any conflicts of interest in who funded the research.

Choosing which research studies to use - are some 'better' than others?

You will want to cite the best possible source of information for the point you are making. There are multiple different ways of designing a research study and each has their strengths and weaknesses. Some people will tell you that there is a 'hierarchy of evidence' and research studies at the top of this hierarchy are better than others. We don't believe that is necessarily true. We believe that all studies have their strengths and weaknesses, and it is the overall pattern of evidence that is important. Certain studies are a better design for certain research questions, but few studies will cover all angles. Again, this is why it is important to read widely around your topic area so that you understand how all the different studies (and their strengths and weaknesses!) fit together.

Randomised controlled trials (RCT) are often considered the 'best' or most rigorous type of research. They recruit people into a study and then randomise them into groups. This theoretically reduces the chances of any other external factors affecting outcomes. For example, if you simply looked at whether people who exercised lived longer your data might be affected by those people who can exercise being healthier in the first place. If you conduct a trial and randomise people to exercise or not, you can then look at the outcomes reducing bias from other factors that might have affected exercise choice.

The problem with RCTs is that they are expensive, difficult to run (how do you encourage or discourage people in your two groups from exercising?!), and often unethical. It's difficult to randomise people to behaviours that could be harmful, for instance you couldn't randomise people to drink 50 units of alcohol a week or not. You can then encounter the issue that people often don't want to take part in trials if they don't get their choice of behaviour, reducing how random your groups are.

RCTs also don't necessarily work well for complex behaviours such as infant feeding. It would be difficult to randomise women to breastfeed or not, in part due to the ethical impacts of that decision but also because we know that breastfeeding is affected by many complex factors. Simply telling a woman she is in a group that is instructed to breastfeed isn't going to work. The RCT design originated in medicine and was typically used to test controllable things like medication dose i.e. comparing outcomes for those randomised to take different doses of a medication.

Finally, RCTs tell us very little about individual experiences within the trial without further research being done. Qualitative work for example often gives context to findings and is just as important. How do people feel about a topic? What factors affect their decision making? What motivates them and what barriers stand in their way? This can be really important data depending on your topic.

This is why it is important to look at a range of research studies when using evidence for your book. What does the data taken from trials say (if available)? What do big cohort studies where they follow people for several decades say? What do experimental studies find? Also, what emerges from surveys, interviews and observations? Importantly what do people who your topic affects say on the subject? What are their lived experiences? This is just as important as hard numbers.

Using systematic reviews and meta-analyses

Often there is such a huge amount of research published on your subject that it can feel daunting, especially if you are coming to the subject from a practice or lived experience perspective with less experience of reviewing academic papers. It is impossible to read everything on a topic area and anyone who claims they have read 'all the research' on a topic, unless it is very obscure, is either lying or simply unaware of just how much has been published. Academics and researchers spend their lives reading papers and yet they are unlikely to ever read all the papers on their expert subject – there are just so many. This is where review papers can be really useful.

There are different types of review paper. Each brings together findings from other papers to consider key themes across them. They differ in terms of how rigorous they are such as how closely they scrutinise the literature, or which papers they include. For example:

- A **narrative review** paper will be more 'informal', tending to not systematically judge each paper included for quality. This doesn't mean it is a poor standard but is often used to more broadly discuss common themes and ideas.
- **Systematic reviews** involve the researchers searching for all published research on a question and looking at what the overall pattern of results say. Often there are limits on what papers are included – maybe in terms of date or location. Typically the strength of the evidence in each paper is judged, considering the methods, sample and limitations of the work. Often more credit is given to the included studies that are considered to be stronger.

If you are writing about health and health policy you will find many important systematic reviews as part of the Cochrane Database. The Cochrane Library is a collection of databases in medicine and other healthcare fields. It holds the collection of Cochrane Reviews which is a database of systematic reviews and meta-analyses summarising and discussing healthcare research.

- A **Meta-analysis** mathematically brings together results from different studies to examine what the data suggests when it is combined. It reduces bias and limitations from different studies.

This means that if meta analyses or systematic reviews are available for your chosen topic, then it is often best to use them. This doesn't mean that you have to discard all the other evidence but it helps reduce the chance of you accidentally finding studies that don't fit with the rest of the bigger picture or cherry picking research studies to fit what you want to say. The authors have done the hard work by scrutinising all the research on the topic and judging its quality. It's still important to read the limitations section of the paper but you can have more confidence in the reliability of the research included.

Can I just refer to my own experience instead?

Maybe you are writing about an area that doesn't have a lot of research published, or what is published has a lot of limitations meaning that it is difficult to find supporting research sources. However, in your practice or experience of working with others you frequently see something occurring. Can you include that?

Absolutely, of course you can refer to your own experience in your book, but you need to make it clear that this is what you are doing. The same goes for informal surveys you have conducted on social media, conversations with others, or observations you have made during activities. These are all valid sources of knowledge but do need to be contextualised and separated from research. This can be as simple as saying 'In my work as a psychologist working with new parents, I often observe that...'. Or 'in an informal survey I conducted on my Facebook page I found...'. Or 'I often notice in conversations with parents I support that they feel...'.

This is especially pertinent for subjects that don't have a lot of research published on specific topics due to underfunding and a lack of real value of the subject area. Although research and evidence is vitally important, just because a research paper doesn't exist doesn't mean that something isn't true. Research is essentially just the documentation of something – albeit hopefully a rigorous and well considered documentation. Things can exist and be true before the research is conducted. But it's vitally important to state where your knowledge has come from so that readers can judge the strengths or limitations of what you are saying. Anecdotes may well be true for an individual, but they are not rigorous data that can be used in helping other people judge whether something applies more widely or is relevant to them.

When is research not research?

With the wide availability of social media, it is easy to conduct a survey on a group you follow and share the findings. This can be a really useful snapshot of what people on the page (who take part) are feeling or experiencing and it is certainly something that you can discuss, noting of course the limitations. It is a good way of sharing individual voices and lived experiences of a topic and can be helpful for 'top tips' / 'what worked for me' examples.

However, it is important to be clear of the differences between asking a few questions on a social media page and well-conducted research. With the rise of researchers using social media to share surveys it can sometimes feel that there is not much difference between a research paper published using this methodology and your social media poll. There are multiple steps taken to conduct a research study that you may not be aware of. These can make a lot of difference to how rigorous and scientific data is – or in other words how well it can be extrapolated to other findings.

Most published research will have been designed using established tools, conducted in a way to try and reduce bias, been subjected to rigorous analysis and then been peer reviewed. Even if a paper essentially finds the same thing as a quick social media survey, we can have more confidence in the data in the paper because it is likely that the sample is more varied, the research questions were less leading and the results subjected to more complex analysis. Certainly there can be limitations to published research but it is likely that more people were involved in scrutinising its conception, design and write up. That's not to say a quick social media survey is useless – far from it. It can help bring your book to life. But it's important to be open that it was a quick survey and be clear about its limitations.

How to understand research papers

Based on the previous guidance, it's likely that if you're writing a non-fiction book that you will end up reading a lot of research papers. Maybe you've got lots of experience in this area but for many people research papers elicit reactions from terror to mind numbing boredom. If you're feeling overwhelmed or unsure as to how to judge and understand the content of a research paper then this section explains what to look for in each section, including some of the ways in which you can judge the quality of the work.

Title

This should describe the paper but double check that it does match the content of the work. Sometimes limitations or context of the research (such as a small sample size of a specific participant group) gets missed out of titles deliberately; or words are added that do not accurately reflect the key findings of the paper at all. Never ever read just the title of a paper and decide it fits with what you need to prove, no matter what it says. Unfortunately too many are inaccurate.

Abstract

The abstract is the summary of the paper that should provide the outline of the research. Abstracts are short and are designed to just include key points. This means that lots of details and limitations can be missing. Use the abstract as a way of telling whether a paper could be useful to read, rather than taking your findings from it. A point of note here is if the paper is behind a paywall please do email the author to ask for a copy. They'd really rather you asked them and had a chance to read it rather than risk citing them inappropriately.

Introduction / background / literature review

This will contextualise the research being conducted in terms of what is already known. This section can be useful in understanding more about the topic and finding new papers to read. Never just directly rely on what is published in this section as being a balanced view of your topic area or an accurate representation of research studies. There is a major problem with researchers reading abstracts / background sections and simply citing statements as fact without going to the actual paper. Please read the actual paper. Also, don't assume that what is presented is the full picture. The authors may have cherry picked studies to suit their argument, leaving out other contrasting work. Yes, even established researchers can be prone to this.

Methodology / methods

This is one of the most important sections of the paper. It should tell you who took part, what they did and how any data was collected and measured. It is vital to read this section in terms of knowing who was involved and what type of study it was. Did they use a questionnaire? Self report? A trial? Where did it take place? Who was excluded, deliberately or due to limited participation?

Another important section to look for is an ethics statement. All research involving humans should have permission from an ethics committee that the study will abide by certain ethical standards including making sure participants have all the information they need to take part, are not being coerced, and have their data kept anonymous. If this is missing what does that say about the study? That they didn't think it was important? That it couldn't get ethical approval? All of these things should raise alarm bells over the potential conduct and issues with a research project.

Results or findings

This section provides the results of the study. It will include details on who took part (compared to who they wanted to ideally take part from the methods). This detail is important to make note of so that you can include any of this detail when writing about the study. So rather than simply saying 'a study found' you can say for example 'a survey conducted with 489 women in Germany'. This gives your writing context so that people can understand more details about the work. You don't necessarily have to do this every single time you write about a study, but it can be helpful in giving depth to the evidence you are sharing so that others can employ their critical thinking skills too.

The main findings will be presented here in terms of statistical tests and qualitative analysis. If you aren't up to speed on statistical outputs and qualitative analysis it can be worth reading about this in more depth so you properly understand the analyses. A good recommendation here is Professor Trish Greenhalgh's book 'How to Read a Paper' which gives a good overview of research methods in different contexts. For reading more about how data is somehow misinterpreted, particularly if you are interested in parenting research we also recommend one of Amy's books 'Informed is best'.

Discussion

This is the section where researchers overview their main findings and link them back to previous research and research gaps. Again, researchers sometimes cherry pick or exclude studies so always keep in mind what they are missing out or not focussing on here. This section should always include a section on limitations of the study which is really important. This is where researchers should highlight limitations with their sample or methods used. It doesn't mean that the paper is 'wrong' or bad research – all research has limitations. But it's important to understand what these are when judging the quality of the study.

How do I know whether a study is high quality or not?

Very few papers are 100% 'bad'. Yes they have limitations in how data was collected, or who took part, and perhaps data could have been collected in a more useful way. The important thing is that these are laid out for you to read, understand and judge for yourself. Again, remember that no one paper should be considered as 'the truth' in isolation. It's all about how the different evidence fits together. So when you are ploughing your way through reading hundreds of papers for your book, know that it's all about helping you see that bigger picture. What is the overall pattern? Where are the gaps still?

When you're reading evidence to support the development of your book you are unlikely to be conducting an intensive review on the quality of each paper. However, there are some questions to keep in mind when you are reviewing research. This is where familiarising yourself with CASP frameworks is useful. CASP stands for the Critical Appraisals Skills Programme and it includes checklists for different types of research to judge how reliable / high quality it is. You can find the checklists for all different kinds of papers from systematic reviews to qualitative work here: https://casp-uk.net/casp-tools-checklists/. Different studies have different designs and therefore quality is checked in different ways. However, some of the common considerations include things like:

- Was there a clear statement of the aims of the research?
- Is the type of methodology appropriate?
- Did the research design suit the aims of the research?
- Did the recruitment strategy suit the aims of the research?
- Did data collection tools suit the research issue and questions?
- Have ethical issues been taken into consideration?
- Was the data analysis sufficiently rigorous?
- Is there a clear statement of findings?
- How valuable is the research?

One of the most important things to think about is the date of the publication. More recent evidence is often considered better as it is more likely to reflect current contexts and to have built on previous research evidence. However, there may also be some really important seminal papers that were ground-breaking at the time, and they certainly deserve to be shared and discussed, even if more recent evidence has moved the field forward. The saying 'standing on the shoulders of giants' comes into play here.

If you do find an older study that doesn't mean it is necessarily now outdated. However, things may well have moved on or changed drastically in that topic area since the research has been conducted. If you find an interesting older paper, it's a good idea to check whether anything more recent has been conducted. We have found that this is particularly true for areas related to health where things tend to change over the years. If there has been new research published, what did they find? How does it fit with the older research? Does it extend it or challenge it?

Just because a newer paper found something different it certainly doesn't necessarily mean that the older paper is now useless. The older paper may have a bigger sample, a more robust research methodology and better analysis. Again, it all comes back to that bigger picture of reading and understanding lots of different research papers in your area.

Most likely you could refer to both, describing what the older study did and how things have now changed (or indeed remain similar). Finally, if the older research is the only research, then it's good practice to point out its limitations of date and how things may have changed.

Be aware of any conflicts of interest

Researchers often require funding to conduct a study, especially if it is a larger study that takes lots of time, has many participants, needs materials, etc. Sometimes they can get funding as part of their university job or from an independent research council. However, often industry wants to conduct and fund researchers to explore specific questions. This means that the industry who are paying for the study would obviously quite like the research to be in their favour.

Now this doesn't mean that researchers will deliberately make up stuff to please the funder. However, it does mean that published research funded by industry is more likely to be in the favour of industry than not. In 2015 Professor Marion Nestle started keeping a log on research published by food and beverage companies around the impact or benefits of their food or related food groups. Of 168 studies that she examined, 156 of them had findings that benefitted the funder[5]. Why? Because often the funder controls what can be published from the study. So if the researchers find no impact (or worse, a negative one) that research is less likely to be published. Conversely, if it finds a positive result, it is more likely to be published, skewing the evidence balance. Sometimes funders also have control over what specifically gets researched and how, meaning that research tools are carefully crafted for the benefit of the industry. We also have to consider that in cases of large and continuous funding that researchers subconsciously want to please those who are paying their salary. This doesn't mean that the researchers are deliberately falsifying data but subtly their preferred outcomes may affect how research questions are shaped and data presented.

This doesn't mean you should just discard anything funded by industry. It just means that you need to be cautious and pay even closer attention to what you are reading.

---

5 https://www.vox.com/2016/3/3/11148422/food-science-nutrition-research-bias-conflict-interest

Chapter 11

Referencing your work

Hot on the tails of our chapter on the importance of evidencing your arguments, comes referencing. In our unofficial survey of authors we know, referencing seems to be one of the most dreaded parts of writing a book. A few years ago, someone asked Lyndsey whether she had read all the references listed in one of her books (there were over 600 of them). She replied 'Of course! They wouldn't be there otherwise'. The question made both of us think. It had never occurred to us that people might not actually read the research paper they were citing in their argument or passage - but it is *so* important.

We have both sometimes sparked curiosity by being able to call to mind specific studies for specific subjects, as if it's some kind of magic party trick. The truth is, if you've spent 30-45 minutes reading and digesting a paper, you are much more likely to remember it. If you *haven't* read it fully then why are you citing it? To really use evidence well you obviously need to read the paper, think about it critically and then apply some interpretive skills.

This will sound obvious to some, and really clunky and fastidious to others. We cannot cherry pick evidence by only reading an abstract or using someone else's reference list and hoping/trusting that *they* have read the evidence. If your name is on the front of the book, you need to be darn sure that the paper you have referenced says what you think it says. We can't tell you how many times we have been frustrated when a speaker, presenter or author misquotes a study – particularly if one of us wrote the paper!

Although this may sound like a challenging amount of work, the trade-off here is that by doing all this reading, your mind will expand and you will be able to recall studies, pieces of evidence and facts that you later come to rely on. Being authoritative in the evidence-based world comes from immersion in the research.

It can be tedious and frustrating to get referencing right but it is one of the most important parts of your book and credibility as an author. Why? For the following reasons:

1. It shows that what you have written is backed up by research evidence rather than just being your opinion alone
2. It allows people to go and check out the details of whatever you have referenced, to check its validity but also read about it in more depth if they want to
3. It is courteous to the researcher / policy maker / original author who created the piece of information and helps avoid plagiarism

The previous chapter covers the importance of the first of these two points – how to understand and use the evidence. Showing where your information has come from and that you have used the best possible evidence is an important part of building your transparency as an author and vital in not spreading inaccurate or false information. The third point is also critically important in terms of being respectful of others who have spent time creating knowledge, and protecting your reputation as a writer. No one wants to be labelled that person who has stolen another writer's ideas and passed them off as their own, even if it was due to naivety rather than intent.

What is plagiarism?

Plagiarism covers a range of different things all linked to inaccurate reporting and citation (referencing) of existing information. At the heart of plagiarism is the act of presenting someone else's ideas and work as your own – whether that's their written, artistic or spoken work. You might do it accidentally, by being careless, or indeed deliberately, hoping that you get away with it. It can be as simple as not citing / crediting someone when writing or speaking about their work, or it can be more in depth where you essentially steal and repackage their ideas under your own name. Actions that could count as plagiarism include:

- Copying lines or images from someone's book, website, social media, or research and not crediting them
- Reading or hearing about someone's work and summarising it in your own words or image without crediting them
- Creating a course based on someone else's book or presentation
- Listening to someone give a presentation and then passing their ideas off as your own

Plagiarising someone is never great, but it can be particularly damaging if you are affecting their work or income by copying their ideas without crediting them. If you see a social media post that they have spent time working on and simply share it without crediting it to them, they are losing out on any benefits such as reputation, connections or income that the post may have brought. If you read someone's book and think 'that's a great idea, I'd like to write a book on that' and simply repackage their ideas without doing your own reading of research literature / adding your own significant experience, then that takes sales and reach away from them and allows you to have an impact with minimal effort which is extremely unfair.

Apart from not being a very nice thing to do, plagiarism can get you into significant trouble. As a university student you can fail an assignment or even be asked to leave the university if you commit (or repeatedly commit) plagiarism. When writing a book, in the worst possible case you could face legal action. Although this is rare, simple accusations of plagiarism or a lack of evidence supporting your arguments can seriously diminish your reputation as an author. You might not be sued but people will avoid supporting your work or you might find it more difficult to publish again.

The good news is that there is a simple way to avoid plagiarism – don't copy the ideas of others! When you do include reference to someone else's research, or writing or a presentation in your work, you need to fairly and credit them. However this doesn't mean that you can simply find someone else's work and stick it all in your writing as long as you add in a tiny number reference that signifies it is based on their work.

If you are using a considerable amount of someone's content in your work you need to stop and think about whether you are simply repackaging (or effectively stealing) their ideas. Including one idea, in a small amount of detail, and clearly stating that it is their idea and that the reader can find out more information by reading their book (insert full title) is good practice. Including several of their ideas or replicating their book or course structure, is not. A book should bring together new ideas and ways of thinking, not simply replicate (copy) something that is out there with a new cover and author name.

To avoid this it is important to be clear on what your distinct book idea is and what expertise / experience you have to write it. That's not to say you can't write a book on a subject if someone else has written one, but you have to make sure that you are not just accidentally or otherwise repackaging their ideas. Your book will need to have novel research conducted, bring novel experience to it, or present differing ideas or evidence to underpin it. Making sure that your work has its own unique selling point, and labour is important, both in terms of avoiding plagiarism and maintaining your credibility. You don't want to be known as that author who stole the work of someone else.

When it comes to referencing someone's work in your book, an important aspect to think about is whether you summarise their ideas or directly quote their work. This will depend on the context of what you are trying to state. If it is a broad concept or idea, summarising in your own words is usually best (while clearly stating it is their idea and where it was published!). However if they have made a specific important point, or rephrasing would be awkward, you can directly quote their work, using speech marks, and subject to a few considerations.

Legally there is no formal word count of the amount you are allowed to quote but know that you should ask permission to use any 'substantial' extract. Unfortunately, there is no hard definition of substantial but in reality this amounts to anything more than a few sentences maximum. If you are quoting less than this you should still clearly state where it came from and use quotation marks to be clear it is their words, for example as Sarah Smith says in her book Parenting in Rainy Weather *'there is no such thing as bad weather, just bad clothing choices'*. This lets the reader know that it is the words of the author but also by adding clear reference to the book it acknowledges their contribution and helps direct readers to their work. Essentially it is a 'payment' of sorts for how they have helped you.

Most authors will be delighted that you are referring to their book and ideas as long as you fairly acknowledge them, use just one small part, and typically paint them in a positive light. It would also be courteous to contact them and let them know you are adding reference to their work in this way and a good form of networking and introduction if you are doing so in a way that supports their work. If you are wondering whether you are fairly using and crediting their work, a good test suggested by the Society of Authors is to reverse the situation and ask yourself whether you would be happy if someone else used your work in this way? No? Then reference and credit others appropriately.

The difference here is when it is a research paper. There is no need to contact every researcher who you include in your book. When it comes to published research you are actively encouraged to include lots of details to contextualise the study for your readers - although do summarise in your own words. Who conducted the research? In what country? What did they do? Who took part? What did they find? What are the limitations? Researchers are reporting their work to the public in order for it to be shared, disseminated and learned from – as long as it is fairly cited as having been done by them.

A quick note here – if you want to use a poem, or song lyrics you actually need direct permission from the songwriter. Yes, even for one short line. Although if you are using it as part of a research study / paper then this is apparently ok. You can however refer to the artist and title of the song. For more consideration on this issue the Society of Authors has a great guideline entitled 'Guide to Copyright and Permissions'[6].

Do I need to reference everything that I write?

This depends on where your information is coming from and the style of the book that you are writing. As detailed in the previous chapter, if you are writing about your own personal experience or your own knowledge gained in practice, then no you wouldn't be expected to cite that. Likewise, if you are using examples of shared common knowledge, rather than pointing to exact research studies, then you may not need to (or be able to cite) that. There are many gaps in our research knowledge, and sometimes what we 'know' hasn't been formally researched yet. However, it is important to make sure you are doing a thorough literature search to make sure you aren't missing something important (see Chapter ten Finding and using research evidence).

When considering whether something needs a reference, think about what you are stating. There is a difference between:

> *'We know that babies wake up lots at night and many continue to do so throughout the first year and beyond'* – **this is general shared knowledge, and a reference is not needed.**

6https://www.societyofauthors.org/SOA/MediaLibrary/SOAWebsite/Guides/Guide-to-Copyright-and-Permissions.pdf

Versus

> *'Research shows that babies wake up most often in the first months of life, but this typically starts to reduce over the coming months. Almost all babies aged 6 – 12 months still wake once or more at least a few times a week'* – **this is specific information and needs a citation and details of the study.**

When considering any information that you feel that you 'just know', it is really important to try to make sure you haven't picked up information from others and forgotten who you learned it from. If you are writing about facts or concepts, it's important to stop and reflect on where the information has come from before presenting it as your own idea.

Finally, if you are referencing research, always make sure that the studies are properly cited. You can't simply write that 'research shows that ...' and not include the link to the reference. It's not a passing fact – it's a study that took considerable time and effort to conduct and report. And of course the proper citation also allows others to read more and check with your interpretation and reporting of it.

How many references will I need?

If you are writing a popular science book, or one that explores historical or political concepts, or a book that is presenting evidence to make a certain point, it is likely that you will need lots of references to support your arguments. However, if you are writing a more practical book, for example one aimed at sleep deprived parents, you may not want to have lots and lots of references for every point you make. They can take away from soothing or helpful messages and advice making it seem overly 'wordy' when the reader has only had three hours sleep.

When Amy wrote her book 'Covid Babies: How Pandemic Health Measures Undermined Pregnancy, Birth, and Early Parenting', she was bringing together evidence around the impacts of the pandemic upon birth and parenting for a wide readership and therefore wanted to clearly back up all her statements. The book is approximately 50,000 words in length with 450 references. Conversely, her much larger manual for new parents 'Let's Talk About the First Year of Parenting' which is 150,000 words long only has 250 references. Clearly a notable difference in what the text looks like in a book but still plenty of references supporting the main points with facts, and most importantly crediting other people's research, experience and ideas.

Even if your book does not include reference to research studies it is unlikely that you aren't making reference to anyone's writing or work in your book. Supporting references can also help to make sure any points that could be challenged have evidence behind them. They are also useful for any reader who wants to use evidence to support their decisions or to show to others, for example parents being able to show doubting family members that their chosen approach to caring for their baby is in fact evidence based.

You can also credit the influences of other people's work by dropping their name and website into your writing. It could be that your target audience is unlikely to want to read detailed references of someone who has conducted lots of research but they might benefit from knowing about their website, blogs and social media which talks about the concepts. If you are referencing a topic they know lots about but not a direct research study you could for example write, 'As Joanna Bloggs talks about so eloquently in her blog entitled *Standing out from the Crowd*...'. If you are referring to people in your book this way, also include their name in the index of your book. Essentially give them as much credit as possible!

Books that aren't heavily referenced also often benefit from a 'further reading list' at the back, or indeed drop references to further sources into your book in appropriate places. This is your opportunity to credit others' work who may have influenced your learning and knowledge over the years, but whom you are not directly citing. It is also good practice to recognise others as important leaders in the field, especially if there are any similarities in topic. Always, always make sure that if there is any chance that you have directly picked up a piece of information from them that you reference them properly.

How do I present references?

There are a number of different formal referencing systems you can use. Each has its own specific rules. Why they are different is not clear. It would really help if they could all sit down together and decide on one sensible way rather than requiring painstaking differences, but until they do it is good practice to pick one referencing style and follow it. The most common referencing systems used in publishing are APA, Chicago, Harvard, and Vancouver.

Your main choice will be whether you refer to articles by author surname and date in the text or a numerical system. The first approach is known as a parenthetical reference and is used in Harvard, APA and Chicago referencing. You then provide a reference list of sources in alphabetical order. The second approach (i.e Vancouver) uses a numerical system. You refer to studies by a number in the text and then provide your references in numerical order in the reference list. For example, taking our own book here:

- Harvard referencing: In 'The Writing Book' the authors stress the importance of accurate and consistent referencing (Brown & Hookway, 2022).
- Vancouver referencing: In 'The Writing Book' the authors stress the importance of accurate and consistent referencing[1].

You can also choose the option of using footnotes but that is far less common and can be distracting if you have more than a few references, although this does depend on subject discipline. For academic work, fields such as psychology tend to use APA, medicine use Vancouver, and history use footnotes – although variations do occur.

The majority of non-academic / mainstream books tend to use a numeric referencing system as it saves on space and is cleaner and easier to read. It's a good idea to check with your publisher in advance what they would prefer you to use. Another thing to think about is whether you will have one long reference list for the whole book, or split references by chapter. It is usually easier to adopt a style where you provide references by chapter otherwise, particularly if you are using a numeric system, your numbers are going to get larger and larger as you go through, taking up more space.

There are further specific rules about how you should present your references in text and in the reference section according to the format you choose. How you present the reference differs according to whether it is a research paper, book / book chapter, policy document or website. Each form also has different rules about how many author surnames you include in the text - the first and second, or whether you can condense by using 'et al'. It is important but mind numbingly boring to follow the rules – and be consistent. Rather than list all the small details here we recommend that you look up the rules of your chosen format.

You can use referencing software which allows you to reference in one format and then switch to another format easily if needed. Many are free but some of the more popular ones such as EndNote and Mendeley have limited storage / options to their free basic versions, with upgrades costing money. Opinion is split about whether these are useful or not. Some people find that the effort they spend entering all the details of the papers into the software in the first place isn't worth it. Others love the organisation. It also depends how much writing you plan to do. If you are managing just a few hundred references it may be less of an issue than if you are juggling thousands.

If you aren't using referencing software a quick tip is to make use of Google Scholar. When you look up a reference it has a quotation mark underneath it. If you click on that it provides the reference in different forms and you can copy and paste it into your reference list.

When should I start compiling my reference list?

One of our top tips to you would be to make sure you keep a note of everything you include in your book as you go along. When you write about a study or piece of evidence, include the reference right from the start. You can then copy and paste the full reference into a separate document or into your referencing software if you use it. Your future self will thank you for doing this as you go along, believe us!

Chapter 12

Editing your work

Once you've got a final draft of your book together you can breathe a sigh of relief. However, unfortunately it's going to have to be a short one as the joy of editing is still to come. We say 'joy' knowing that while some people tolerate editing or even enjoy polishing their work, others simply hate it. They hate going back over what they have written and are desperate to just be finished and press send to their editor.

We'll admit - editing is a difficult and time-consuming job. However, learning to edit your work well will also add considerably to your writing skill, as well as make your editor's / proof reader's / very kind friend's life easier! Don't be tempted to skimp on this task even if you are sending it to an editor. There will be parts you have missed and although editors work magic, they won't always spot specialist content that is missing because you are the expert here, not them.

Editing involves checking for tone, sense, flow and readability. It also obviously includes checking for spelling, grammar and typographical errors. Make sure any acronyms are written in full the first time, and you give a full description of anything that needs explaining the first time you introduce it rather than later on in the work. For example if you describe a technical term, policy or concept make sure the explanation is attached to the first introduction and not later in the book. Also check aspects such as where you refer to another chapter and that you haven't inadvertently written notes to yourself such as 'needs more detail' and not gone back to add it.

You may also need to reduce words, check your references are accurate and ensure your tenses are consistent throughout. When you read through your draft you may also realise that you've missed out topics that need to be included or indeed repeated yourself and can now reduce those sections. Essentially it's all about looking at your book as a big picture and how it hangs together rather than considering chapters in isolation. You may need to signpost readers more or tell them that things are coming up later.

Editing is an important aspect of your work because nobody wants to plough doggedly through long, inarticulate or complex paragraphs. As a writer, you are a professional storyteller – irrespective of whether the story you have to tell is fiction or non-fiction. Reading should be pleasurable – even if it is for a purpose. We're not suggesting that you need to pepper your text with jokes, but consider the attention span, varying intellects and headspace of your reader. You are a literary servant – delivering your meaning like waiting staff deliver food. Make it appealing, appetising and get to the point efficiently and enjoyably.

It can help to take a short break in between finishing your book and doing any editing. This gives you a chance to have a break, step back and clear your mind so that you can come back with fresh eyes. Some people just need a day or two, others might need a little longer. Sometimes it can help to build in thinking time away from your computer. Some long walks / time spent in nature, an activity that distracts your body such as swimming, or simply doing something completely different for a few days gives your brain time to calm down. It's often during periods of relaxation or distance from our work that we get the most inspiration.

You might like to send your draft to a trusted friend. Think carefully about who you send it to because on the one hand they need to be invested enough to actually read a giant document, but also distant enough to be able to offer criticism that you will accept constructively. Your partner may have the dedication to you but are you really ready to openly listen to how they think your sentence structure needs improving? Probably not.

One tip is to print out your work, although we realise this can be expensive and is not the environmentally friendly option. However evidence shows that we have a tendency to miss errors more on a screen than we do on paper. If you are self-publishing you can order yourself a proof copy of your finished book to read through and the larger publishing companies may print you a proof of your book for the final editing stage - although at that stage you probably aren't going to be able to make many changes. It's hard to describe exactly why but for some reason holding your work in your hand can be so helpful in really getting the feel of your book and seeing it in a different way.

Also, consider how your book will sound when read aloud. Increasing numbers of people want to listen to audio books. Audiobooks are typically recorded word for word and making sure that your writing 'sounds right' spoken out loud is a specific skill. A long sentence might look ok on paper but leave you, or your reader, gasping for breath when narrated. Read a paragraph out loud to yourself every few pages and check that it sounds as good as it reads.

Finally, if you are dyslexic or neurodiverse it's worth exploring whether there may be any financial support you can apply for, through grants or Access to Work (UK specific but check if your country has something similar), which may support you with someone to help with proofreading. Some people are unaware that the Access to Work service covers aspects such as note taking, proofreading and coaching and may be available if you had a diagnosis of ADHD, autism or dyslexia. Find out more at: https://www.gov.uk/access-to-work/eligibility

Conveying your ideas in shorter pieces

Another challenge for editing your work crops up if you are asked to write an article based on the concepts in your book, or you need to talk about the work on social media, or in a press interview. Chapters 15 and 16 deal with the more practical aspects of engaging with others through presentations and the media, but how do you go about condensing your work if asked to?

After the work of writing a book, you might at first glance feel like writing shorter pieces is easier. In fact though, the stakes are often higher. More people may potentially read a short piece of writing than a 300-page book. Lyndsey once joked to Amy that she was going to complete her PhD in memes. Obviously she wasn't serious, but the serious point within the joke here is that it is likely that thousands of people will see a graphic on social media that articulately conveys a point, versus a hundred or so who read some of the nerdier academic articles. Short pieces of writing are thus a huge opportunity to tell a potentially much larger audience about your work.

But how on earth do you summarise your life's work in a meaningful way? If you have submitted articles for publication you have a bit of a head start here, as you normally need to write an abstract of 150-300 words which can sometimes be very daunting. Even if you have experience with taking a pair of metaphorical shears to a monster piece of work it is quite a fine art to be that succinct, and yet still meaningful.

By now, you've hopefully had a chance to think about your book audience. You need to do the same with your article or post. Who will read this? Are they your usual audience, or are they likely to be more critical? Will they need a softer approach? Do they need convincing? Do you need to pack a punch with some weighty evidence? Or do you need to simplify a complex message? Working this out helps plan your article. Here are some hints to get you started:

- Think about what conclusion you want your reader to end up with after reading your piece.
- With your end conclusion in mind, think about how you break this down into an introduction, main body and conclusion.
- In your introduction, you frame the context of your problem or argument. This should usually be a fairly small proportion of your word count.
- The main body of your article is where you basically make your case. This works best if you sub-divide this into a few clear key points. Depending on the subject, perhaps these are the likely objections to your argument, or maybe they are the factors influencing it. Each key point needs to be succinctly explained.
- Your conclusion should neatly wrap up your article and leave your reader with a final thought, somewhere they can go to read more, or a concluding statement.

Even if you think you are being succinct, it can take a lot of practice to convey your message coherently. At times, you will almost certainly have to sacrifice paragraphs and additional words. Here's how to get your word count down:

- Critically scrutinise your writing for any superfluous description. If it's not essential to make your point, it can go.
- Check for use of expletives. Getting rid of these is a really easy way to lose words without meaning and it makes your writing cleaner too. Expletives are words like 'very', 'exceptionally', 'drastically', and so on. They are often used to add emphasis but they're a bit of a luxury when you have a tight word count and removing them usually doesn't affect the tone or message.

- Depending on where this your work will be published, you may be able to use contractions and hyphenate words. Contractions are shortened words made by blending two words together - such as were not becoming weren't, did not is didn't, and so on. This is often not appropriate for academic writing but if you've been asked to write a piece for a magazine you can probably get away with it.

- Read through your work and consider whether any sentences could be rephrased in a less wordy way.

- Check for repetition. Sometimes repetition is deliberate, as it adds emphasis, or serves as a reminder. However, this is less necessary in a short article as people usually do not need these reminders. Repetition is an obvious way to add unnecessary words and therefore this is quite an easy way to get your word count down.

- Ask someone else to help you cut words. It is almost counter-intuitive at first to remove words. After all, you probably wrote the word for a reason. We can become emotionally attached to the ways in which we explain a concept. This is why someone else can sometimes come in and successfully and unemotionally carve out sections that do not add much to the overall meaning. To you it may be brutal, but to someone else it feels logical.

Here is an example of a section of writing that has been heavily edited to reduce the word count by half:

Version 1:

Very often when writing, there is so much to say about your particular special interest topic that it can feel almost impossible to articulate your meaning succinctly, without losing the tone and meaning of the passage. Editing the words down to within the allowable word count can feel counterintuitive at best, and brutal at worst. But with clever editing, the meaning is not lost and in fact, you may end up with a better-worded passage of writing than the one you started with. Being succinct and concise does not mean losing all the heart and soul of your writing - it just means avoiding excessive words and in some cases, re-phrasing sections to avoid wordiness. (114 words)

Version 2:

> *Difficulties in succinctly articulating a complex topic are common. Editing words to within the allowable limit can feel brutal. However, clever editing avoids loss of tone and leads to a better-worded passage. Being concise does not mean losing the soul of your writing - it just cleans your writing, often through re-phrasing wordy sections. (53 words)*

Editing words down is tedious in many ways but it will often finesse your writing style if you practice this frequently. Try it with random passages you pull from the internet - can you get the word count down while retaining the meaning? Give it a go - you'll be amazed at how this will improve your ability to polish a paragraph, and write succinctly.

Final checks

One of the earlier tasks is to sign off on the book cover, blurb, author bio, edits and layout of your book. You will be involved in many of these aspects although if your work is being published, some of these jobs will be coordinated or steered by your publisher. You are likely to have to check over the edited version of your manuscript. This is often a PDF copy of your book. Clearly, when you create your manuscript in a word processing application, this will be a different layout to the final book version. It can be quite a lot of work to format the chapters and lay the book out so that the headings are in sensible places. This is called book interior layout and believe it or not there are experts in the field who are masters at designing books on the inside.

Laying out books on the inside involves editing the font size, paragraph spacing, consistency of headings and chapter titles, making sure that any tables and diagrams appear in a sensible place and so on. So, when you see your book in this format it is likely to look quite different and is the first glimpse of how it will appear to your reader. This change is often quite helpful because when you see your words looking slightly different on the page it can help you more easily spot errors you'd like fixed before it goes to print. This is a job that requires sharp eyes because occasionally you will spot an error, typo or something that has been edited too heavily.

You may also, on re-reading, discover that something that made sense to you at the time suddenly feels like it requires further explanation or clarity. You may wish to cite another hot-off-the-press article to bring your manuscript right up to date or rephrase something. At this point in the proceedings, it's best to check with the publisher if you want to make a major edit, as the book may already have a provisional layout. If you add a lot of words this can affect the layout of the book and may mean that the subsequent chapters or headings are shifted. Laying out a book is an intense and lengthy task which means it may not be possible to make any major alterations if you leave this until the last moment.

You may also be asked to help your editor finalise the blurb on the back of your book. You might find the sections about abstracts for presentations in Chapter 15 helpful for this, but essentially the blurb may make the difference between someone buying your book, or putting it back on the shelf. It will be some of the most important words you ever write, even if it's one of the shortest pieces!

One of the more exciting parts of getting your book ready for printing is finalising the cover. Your publisher may ask if you have any ideas for a cover and then a designer or artist will be commissioned to create some options for you both to review. It is unusual to like the first cover you lay eyes on, so don't despair if you are not wowed by the first draft. Remember that this is your book, so while the publisher may have some specifications about some aspects of the book cover, especially if it is part of a series, you do have some influence. Of course, if you are self-publishing you will have 100% control over aspects like this though you will also be funding the cost of a graphic designer or artist - and multiple revisions can add to the time (and therefore money!) it takes them to finalise your product.

Whether you have chosen the traditional publishing or self-publishing route, you will also need a brief author biography which may be positioned on the first few inner pages, as well as on Amazon, your publisher's page, and your website if you have one. Take your time over this as you want to make sure you are giving an accurate and appropriate account of yourself. There is more information about this in Chapter five.

Once these checks, edits and final proofs are complete, your book will either be sent for printing, or some publishers print on demand. Either way, at this point, it will be difficult or impossible to amend. If you are self-publishing and printing on demand you have more flexibility of course, but it is stressful to keep making changes. At some point, you may have to learn to know when it is finished.

Chapter 13

Publication and promotion

So, you've written your book and now you can sit back and relax whilst the sales, accolades and fame and fortune roll in, right? Sadly most likely not... (sorry). Raising awareness of your book's existence and persuading people they need it in their lives (and keeping that momentum going) are large parts of ensuring your carefully crafted work is read. This is unfortunately going to involve some concerted effort on behalf of yourself, and your publishers if relevant. We say 'unfortunately' because we are very aware that not everyone enjoys the process of marketing their work but hopefully this chapter will a) give you some ideas of how to tackle this, and b) help you feel more comfortable to do so.

Marketing a book is a lot of work. How much work you will have to do to get your book visible depends on how well known you and your work are, whether you have a social media presence, whether you have self-published or have been published by a publishing house, and if it's the latter, how big the publisher is and their marketing budget. Yikes - that's a lot of variables! What does that have to do with you? Well, you can't expect a publisher to do *all* the work. To some extent, if you write an amazing book, word of mouth will get it so far. Even then, you will find that you need to put some effort into continual marketing of your book. Unless you have written a book of epic Stephen Hawking influence, it is likely to need a bit of help to become known.

The thing is – *you* know how good your book is. Your publisher does too. But everyone else is frankly going to judge your book by its cover, blurb and whatever marketing and reviews it has had. It's going to need a leg up otherwise it will be floundering down at the bottom of the book sales rankings. Many people overestimate how well their book will sell, assuming that everyone in their target audience will know about it and buy the book. But this simply isn't the case. People need to know about it in order to want to buy it.

You might feel that it is your publisher's job to market your book for you. After all, they took the book on and they're the ones with the book budget. Of course, it *is* a publisher's job to market your book and they have a vested interest in making sure it does as well as it can. Often though, the best person to sell your book is.... you. You know your book better than anyone else. You know the people who will read it. You know what they should be getting out of it. You know the best bits! It is absolutely part of your job as a writer to promote your book, and often the more effort you put in, the more people will find out about (and buy) your book. Both of us have watched this happen with our own books - as we step up our engagement, book sales follow.

The importance of writing a good press release

A really useful tool when announcing your book is to write a press release about its imminent launch. If you are being published by a publishing company they may take the lead on the press release, though they may still ask for your input. If you are self-publishing you may want to write your own press release.

Writing a press release is a particular skill. It needs to cover what your book is about, why it has been written and who should read it... all in as few words as possible so people will actually read it. One side of A4 max is usually enough and that would include space for headlines, the book cover, your photo and short bio. Commonly, a book release will include the following:

- What the book is about
- What its key messages are
- Why your book topic matters
- Who the book is aimed at and who should read it
- A short bio about you i.e., who you are and what your expertise is that has led you to write this book
- Who is publishing it / where people can buy it
- How people can contact you

If you have a publisher it is likely that they will send out the release to different book publishing, subject specialist and media contacts. They may ask you if you have a list of any contacts that you would like added to a release. If you do not have a publisher you can launch your own media release in different ways including sharing on your social media, sending to useful contacts (don't spam everyone in your address book from your distant fourth cousin to your favourite Chinese restaurant though). You can boost the announcement of your book by creating short videos about its content for social media, having an 'unveiling' event, or releasing a short article with an extract of your book in it (check with your publisher about any of these things if relevant).

There are various press release websites you can now sign up to. Some of these are free but bear in mind that everyone who wants something to hit the media will also be making use of this. You can also pay for it to be promoted to interested journalists and organisations. There are a range of prices and services but before you invest, do think carefully about a) whether journalists would really be interested in your story and b) even if they are, whether it would be worth it for sales figures. You certainly don't need the media to be interested in order to sell lots of copies of your book. Sending details of your release to a carefully selected group of subject specialist contacts (who you've spent time networking and developing relationships with) is probably a lot more beneficial - and cheaper.

Promoting your book

It's possible that if you are working with a larger publisher and / or your book is expected to sell very well, then you might be asked to go on a book launch tour speaking at different events. This is obviously a fantastic, albeit time consuming opportunity. However, this typically only happens for books predicted to have considerable reach. If you think about how much profit your book sales will bring and balance that across the cost of arranging events then you can see how sales would need to be considerable to make this worth the effort.

A more likely outlet for promotion is the media. If you have a publisher they will likely have some contacts in the media world, and will probably try to line up interviews, podcasts, or articles for you. Alternatively you may have built up media contacts over the years and will be directly able to approach potential outlets yourself. These opportunities are often worth taking although judge each individual one as to relevance and audience. What you don't want to risk doing is working with an outlet that is not well received in your subject area. Although 'there's no such thing as bad publicity' is a common phrase this, sadly, isn't always true.

Getting your book into the right magazine or newspaper or onto a relevant website is often a brilliant way to raise awareness of your book outside your immediate social circle though. There are a number of ways this can happen. Sometimes a magazine or website will agree to write a review of your book which is obviously a brilliant direct promotional tool. Typically they are more likely to do this for books that closely match the ethos of their publication as they want readers to think it is relevant. More mainstream or larger outlets also tend to focus predominantly on books with larger sales figures.

What is more likely to happen is that they ask you to write an article or other piece for them, typically free of charge. This is an excellent opportunity as it promotes your book but also yourself as an expert in your subject area. They may allow you to include links to your website or social media alongside your book details, so that people can contact you more easily.

It is likely that if you work with someone else then they will have clear ideas on the topics you write and talk about. Although they may simply promote your book for you, they know that their readers / viewers follow them for a reason - for content. View this as a mutually agreeable exchange. They offer you their platform and audience and you offer them an interesting expert piece in return. You can get ahead here and have a crib sheet of possible talk outlines, or skeleton articles for newspapers and magazines.

Often magazines want you to write an article that has practical use for readers such as 'The 5 Myths Everyone Needs to Know About X...', 'Top Tips for Problem Y', or 'How to do Z in Ten Steps'. So plan ahead for this. You can have a number of short articles or blogs of around 500-800 words that you can edit slightly for different outlets. This might save your sanity because journalists often want an article turned around in 24 hours, especially if they are asking you to write in relation to a topical news issue, so there's rarely a lot of time to slowly deliberate over a piece. It has to be ready to go.

Think about what topics in your book are appealing to different audiences. What does your audience often need help with? What issues do they find interesting? What gaps in knowledge do you think they need to know more about? Make a list, ensuring that the titles appeal to your audience. Editors of magazines will want to know that your piece will increase sales / reputation of their publication. It costs money to print / publish a piece and you are essentially ensuring increased readership of their publication in exchange for access to their platform and readers.

It's also possible that you will be asked to provide a media interview related to your book content if it happens to align with current news stories. We have more detail on this in Chapter 16, but one tip is to have a draft of the key messages (e.g. soundbites) in your book already prepared so you don't panic if you suddenly get a media call. On the subject of media relevance, it can also help to have some articles ready to go so that when a media story hits you can edit it for relevance to the story and publish rapidly. Of course you'd need a crystal ball to predict some news stories but you most likely know what topics frequently rear their head, or are bubbling under the surface in your subject area.

Finally, you might also get asked to contribute an article, do a social media takeover, or conduct a 'live' on a social media page or for a social media influencer. Some Facebook and Instagram pages have huge followings of people who might be your target audience, these can be a great way of letting people know that there's a new book on the block (see Chapter 14 for more information about how to use social media to boost your book). You could offer to write a piece / do a live for a social media page but be nuanced in who you approach. It helps to have a relationship with a page beforehand, and to make sure that what you are offering will be beneficial to them too; otherwise it can feel like you are taking advantage of them and even put them off promoting your work further down the line.

When choosing which pages and influencers to work with you do need to be really careful. There is a huge trend at the moment in using influencers with very large followings to promote and advertise products, services or books. Marketers have cottoned on to the fact that many people trust the opinion of certain individuals more than a cold advert. Because of this, many influencers have agents and you might have to go through someone else, or even pay to have them endorse your book.

Influencers can be a very effective way to let a lot of people know about your book. But this comes with a warning. Make sure the person you approach has values that align with yours, and ensure there are no ethical hang-ups. Who else have they worked with? Do they collaborate with a brand you don't approve of? Have they done any paid partnerships with unethical companies? Have they made racist, offensive, or homophobic remarks? It's a real minefield, so make sure that you do your research.

It is unlikely that a large social media page will approach you unless they are aware of your reputation and work (although of course, you might pique their interest with your work). Having a clear social media strategy whereby you build your connections and raise awareness of your profile before launching your book can help increase the likelihood of you being invited onto their page.

Organising a book launch

Another great form of promotion is a book launch. If you have a publishing deal it is likely that your publisher will want to discuss a launch, although how big an occasion, or how formal, are very dependent on your publisher. You may have a face to face event with champagne, invited guests and book signing. Or you may launch it as part of another event or conference, or even online. Remember that you can plan a series of smaller events face to face and online - and at different times of the day to reach a broader audience.

Although online launches may feel less celebratory they can be really useful in terms of accessibility and reach - for those in a different country or time zone, or who may not be able to easily attend a physical event. It also gives you an opportunity to record it and share it afterwards to reach even more people. If you link it to social media you will appeal to an even wider range of people - many of whom love the idea of watching you talk about your book but may never have considered themselves to be the book launch 'type'.

Some ideas for an online book launch content include:

- Simply spending time talking about why you wrote your book
- Reading a chapter of your book
- Giving a presentation about a key topic
- Setting up an interview where you are asked questions about your book, perhaps by someone well known in your field
- Having a panel presentation on a theme
- Asking potential readers to send in questions for you to answer

Sometimes, a book launch can feel underwhelming or anticlimactic after all the work leading up to this. You might feel exhausted, shell shocked or fed up of thinking about the book but take this opportunity for one last push as it really can help with the promotion and spread of awareness of your work. You can always host a smaller event with closer friends and family or simply go out for a celebratory meal. Whatever you do, we strongly encourage you to allow yourself to feel rightly proud of yourself. Remember to celebrate you and what you have achieved aside from all the book promotion.

Other forms of book promotion

Not everyone will have the opportunity to work with the media. This isn't because your book is not interesting but perhaps that it is not relevant to the outlets at that time. They may have run similar stories recently or feel that your book or subject wouldn't have a large enough appeal. Your work can also get overshadowed by major media events. Amy has lost count of the number of times when she has had a media piece lined up and it's been bumped to later or discarded completely because of a breaking news story. Unfortunately the media's tendency to follow current events can work both ways - sometimes you'll catch the wave of a story because your topic is suddenly relevant and at other times they'll look straight past you.

This is obviously disappointing but it is by no means the end for your book promotion. You can have a significant impact and reach yourself, although we won't lie - you need to be prepared to put in the time, thinking and possibly money to make this happen. At the core of this is thinking about wherever you happen to be active, have a community, loyal fans, clients and followers - these might be physical or digital locations. Here are some other platforms that you may wish to consider to promote your book. Each of these has different costs involved (whether that's financial or time based) so working creatively within your budget is important. You might find that you have to experiment a little to establish what works best for you.

- Attend relevant conferences, fairs, and study days
- Work with other businesses who have physical premises / classes
- Collaborate with other authors to promote each other's work
- Pay to promote books using social media 'boost' or sponsored ad functions. You can also pay to promote books on Amazon

- Send books to trusted and respected professionals to review. Your publisher may do this - if they don't, ask whether you can have some free or discounted copies to send to people
- Donate books to charities for prizes or do a social media giveaway
- Sell signed copies of your books and set up special discount codes for followers to directly buy them from you

Remember to respond to and encourage people who photograph themselves reading your book. Don't ever think that someone has too small a following if they've taken the time to buy, read and praise your book. Thank them and share their posts - a double bonus of both being a kind and grateful author and sharing photos of your book.

As is the case when working with the media, it can help to offer people something in return for promoting your book to them. Write articles, blogs and social media posts about key themes, linking to your book for further information. Set up a website full of your resources. Send a newsletter out which keeps people updated on key happenings in your subject area. Although it can feel like you are giving away free information, this really is a 'speculate to accumulate' situation. People feel far less like they are being advertised to if you drop in a link to your online shop after writing a useful blog or interesting newsletter than they do if you simply spam them with book promotion posts. They also share free stuff they enjoy which helps to promote your reputation and expertise more broadly. There is more on using social media to promote your work in the next chapter.

Whichever way you choose to promote your book, you will need to plan to do it regularly because there is so much competition within each book genre and subcategory - people need to be reminded of how good yours is. It's an obvious point but people are constantly training or at different life stages, therefore the people who knew about your book a month ago are not the same people today.

Remember, people have busy lives. While your book is at the front of your brain, we can guarantee that they will forget your name, forget the title of your book, and forget that they even thought about your book. So you need to remind them (gently). Just think about yourself for a moment. How often have you seen an advert for a TV show, book, product or movie that really piqued your interest? Then a few hours later when you're relaxing, you furiously rack your brain trying to remember what it was. You're human, and so is everyone else.

However there is a fine line between self-promotion and over promotion. It is unbearable when people endlessly go on about their book, or do nothing except promote their book. As long as you're mixing it up, you should be ok. It can be pretty difficult to tell the difference between promoting your book and driving everyone round the bend. Those who are struggling with impostor syndrome may especially believe that everyone is bored of hearing about their book. But honestly, mostly this is a lack of confidence talking. If you are mixing up your content then it's unlikely that people will get fed up and move on - they will simply scroll past the book promotion and wait for different content.

Finally, one thing to bear in mind is whether there is any conflict of interest or potential unhappiness from your employer (if you have one) in promoting your book or the way that you do it. Some people are unable to talk about their published book while at work, of perhaps their topic is not relevant to their paid work. Other employers may value what you do and encourage you to share your work widely. It's a good idea to give some thought as to whether your manager (if you have one) would be ok with you talking about, or promoting your book in a public setting.

Your little black book

Another really important way of promoting your book is to build up your network of professional contacts. This serves multiple purposes. Firstly, you can collaborate with other professionals who might find your book a helpful resource. Perhaps you work in a field where clients tend to collaborate with allied professionals for holistic, joined up care. Meeting and establishing relationships with these professionals can increase the reach of your book, and also build up a community of people all invested in developing services that meet the needs of your client group.

Secondly, if more professionals know about your book, they will be able to recommend it to colleagues or clients. Many professionals are grateful to know that someone they can trust has written a great resource that they can recommend as an evidence-based source. This saves them time and improves the care they are able to offer. Thirdly, this can create a useful source of cross-referrals. If you refer families, clients, or followers to your trusted circle of professionals, this obviously supports other local businesses. They are also more likely to recommend their clients to you and your book. Finally, we learn from each other. It's not possible to be an expert in everything - your professional contacts may be able to fill the gaps in your knowledge, and vice versa.

Networking can also be a really good way of making connections with media, journalists, creative designers, and all manner of wonderful people whose services might be exactly what you need. The connection of course is likely to be mutually beneficial and, as with all relationships, you should go into these looking for ways to help others out as much as they might be able to help you.

Networking can be about more than just trying to get a foot in the door somewhere – it should be about making meaningful connections and building a community. How do you make these connections? Well, you could start with asking around for personal recommendations. You could also try the Writers & Artists Yearbook, published - funnily enough - every year. This is a huge directory of services and professionals within the writing and literary world. Another option is to scour the web pages of the organisations where the professionals you are interested in may be members. They may have a registry or a country contact / chair.

Attending conferences is a great way to network, and many of these connections are mutually beneficial (see Chapter 15 for more about the advantages of presenting and speaking at conferences). If you work in a specific field you could keep an eye on relevant Facebook groups, Instagram pages and even the authors of peer reviewed papers to see who seems to be a credible or influential contact that you'd like to nurture. You can also try a good old fashioned quick and dirty Google search but this comes with a warning, just because someone is on the first page of your search, does not necessarily mean they are credible – they may just have really good search engine optimization (or have paid someone to do that).

It also helps to see networking as a long game. It takes years or even decades to develop a large network. The good news though is that the early stages are the most intensive. As your reputation and network grows, proportionately you will likely spend less time maintaining it. The early effort really is worthwhile. It's a little like creating a garden from scratch - hard work, time consuming and little immediate reward but in years to come you'll start to see the rewards with minimal input (aside from occasionally weeding out connections that are no longer useful).

Coming out of your shell (how to cope if you're shy)

If you have read this chapter and now have a thin sheen of sweat on your upper lip, or have a strong desire to crawl into a cave and stay there, fret not. One of the things you will need to get over is the cringe factor about promotion. If you're struggling, it can be helpful to learn to think the following thought process:

Why did you write your book in the first place?

- *Because it's going to help people be better informed / more confident / well equipped or (fill in the blank)*

How will people know about this wonderful resource unless you tell them all about it?

- *You need to tell them, otherwise you are denying them the opportunity of learning or growing.*

There are lower key ways of marketing your book that do not involve having your face on a giant placard at a local fair. To an extent you have to expect some attention if you write a book. In order to sell your book you will have to overcome a fear of talking, unless you plan to write your book purely for the experience of doing so.

- Pre-record videos rather than do live videos
- Focus on social media marketing with memes, pictures, quotes and infographics to share your key messages
- Get others to provide reviews of your book (and obviously repay this favour if possible)

As above, give people something in exchange for your promotion. It feels far less cringey to write a useful social media post for people linking subtly to your book than it does to wave your book in their face

Sometimes you just have to be brave, get out there, talk about your book or your work, and then retreat. If you're an introvert and find it scary and intimidating to be the focus of attention, then frankly you're in good company. Many authors and writers have to become chameleons, coming out of their shells to do what they have to do, before escaping to solitude. See it as part of your job and just like any job there are parts you do not enjoy, but can be time limited. Treat your first few nerve-wracking live talks or podcasts as you would a visit to the dentist - possibly uncomfortable, not great to look forward to, but certainly better in the long run.

An approach that can help with this is to develop an author persona separate to every day you - almost like an actor would develop a character for a film. We don't mean start talking about yourself in the third person but rather have a stage approach so to speak. Any mistakes, criticism or things you'd simply like to do differently are all associated with stage you, rather than everyday you. What traits do you want the stage version of yourself to have? Are you confident? Like talking to people? Really caring? This might sound a little crazy but trust us and try it out, it can really work.

You will also probably find that over time your fear of publicity eases. The first few 'appearances' are always the most nerve wracking. If you can keep in mind that it will get easier over time, this can help persuade your brain to get through the fear. It can sometimes help to build up the scale of what you do, starting small and testing out your presentation skills on a smaller podcast or magazine. Then you can start gradually building up to the bigger pieces once you've gained more confidence. If you are savvy about it, you can start experimenting with public speaking and engagement long before your book comes out, so that by the time it's out there, you've gained much needed confidence.

Basically, whether you accept you will have to fake it, or you can pull it out of the bag for a brief moment, we promise you it's worth persevering. After all, you've written a great book – the world needs to know about it!

Coping with publication day

After all the work of promotion and preparation, publication day may have crept up on you. You might still have several jobs on your hands that you need to address before your book hits the shelves. As 'P-Day' approaches you may experience all the feels including a mixture of:

- **Nerves.** Even for more experienced authors with numerous publications, it is common to be nervous about how your book will be received. You don't have to have written about a particularly controversial topic to feel sick to your stomach at the thought of it being published and people reading it.

- **Anxiety.** It is also common to feel anxious as you await your book's reception. Waiting for those first reviews, wondering how many turn up to the book launch, and how well your book sells are all very normal aspects to feel anxious about.
- **Excitement.** For many people, publishing a book represents a dream they have nurtured for a long time, not to mention all the hard work of writing the book.
- **Pride.** Seeing your book in print for the first time is undoubtedly a proud moment, and you deserve to enjoy that feeling. Celebrate!
- **Relief.** After the work of researching for, writing, editing and checking your book, you might feel glad that the hardest part is over.
- **Sadness.** Perhaps although the book was hard work, it also gave you a meaningful purpose. Many people feel a bit of a gap when the writing part of their life is complete. We're not going to lie - one option if you suffer with after-book blues is to write another book...

Sometimes publication day can feel like a bit of an anticlimax and you might even feel a bit empty. This is a completely normal reaction and one that will likely pass. Sometimes we build up publication day as this amazing event in our book's life. Of course it can be, but in other ways it is really just the start of your book's journey. It's more like a celebration of your first job than a retirement party. It's hopefully got a long life ahead of it with many exciting opportunities to come - this is just day one! From personal experience as well, we would suggest you don't expect to get much done on publication day. Not only is it a just cause for celebration, but all the complex emotions you are likely to feel will probably put an end to any significant productivity. Just try to enjoy the day, and soak up the rightly deserved praise.

At this point it's pertinent to remind yourself of realistic sales figures (go back to Chapter six if you need a recap) but to also know that immediate sales figures are not always a key indicator of success. Don't take too much notice of pre-order or even first month figures. Although your close friends and followers might pre-order your book, or jump to buy it on publication day, others are going to want to wait to see whether it is any good or not, especially if this is your first book. As your book becomes better known and more people start promoting and discussing it, opportunities to promote it may start to snowball and sales are likely to grow. Pace yourself and play the long game.

Chapter 14

Social media

Whether you're a big fan of social media or not, admitting that it can be very useful for book promotion and sales is unfortunately necessary. We're going to assume that you have a social media page. Or at least that you realise that if you're in any way trying to target people who use their phone every day, then social media is an effective way to reach certain people.

Why? Well, whether you like it or not, social media is where it's at. It's where we see breaking news. It's where we stay in touch with people. It's where we are kept up to date with the latest goodness / badness / weirdness out there in our respective worlds. While there are some people who hate social media, and avoid it at all costs, for many, it is part of everyday life. Unless you are in a very niche field with a target audience who all happen to hate social media, it is likely that social media could boost sales of your book at least to some extent.

These days, many people report that the primary way they generate leads, sales or clients is through social media. So if you're not on social media or not making it work for you then you're missing out on firstly, spreading the good information that you have to share, secondly, generating meaningful income, and thirdly, becoming known as a credible resource.

Like it or not, people look to influencers on social media. The general public do not necessarily realise that the person with 500 followers might be vastly more qualified and credible than the person with 1.2 million followers. Sadly, that's just the world we live in. So for a time you may feel like a small fish in a very, very large ocean, and an ocean full of sharks and fishing boats at that. Do take heart - even the smallest fish can make waves and challenge the sharks.

If you really do dislike social media or feel completely overwhelmed by the prospect, the good news is that there are plenty of social media experts around that you can hire - although they will obviously charge you. You might decide this is worth the investment as part of your longer-term plan, or you might take the approach of slowly developing your own skills. Remember that different social media pages will have different audiences. Although you can look to people you admire for inspiration, it's important not to blindly follow one way of engaging, especially if it feels uncomfortable. Your social media page should reflect you, your strengths and your work. For example, as an academic sharing research-led information on her social media pages, Amy feels totally at home presenting a critique of a research paper but you're highly unlikely to find her doing a comical dance in an Instagram reel.

So what approach should you take and how can you develop your skills and grow your audience? We are by no means social media experts but we've learned a thing or two as we've grown our fairly respectable followings over the last few years. Here are our top tips:

1. Make your page a place people want to hang out

We cannot tell you how many people message us specifically to tell us that they come to our pages over others because they know that spending time on our grids will make them feel better. Be uplifting - this makes people feel good. Make your page a place where people exhale and feel they have found their people. One of the ways you can do that is simply by being yourself. Whether that's being a lovable nerd, creating amazing dance reels or showing your warts-and-all real life, if you are authentic and real the right people will gravitate towards you.

Be realistic in who will want to follow you. You won't be for everyone. Own that. It's absolutely ok to not try to be all things to all people. There are so many accounts to follow, but what people want is to connect with people they can relate to.

It's also important to take a no shaming stance – this makes people feel safe. While some people swear by conflict and inflammatory statements to divide opinion, this can be a high stress strategy. Sure, there are times when you have to stick to your word. After all, if you don't stand for something, you'll fall for anything. But if your entire social media strategy is based around criticising others, people will look for a place that feels less stressful!

2. Professionalism

If you're trying to grow a business using social media as a platform, another important aspect is professionalism – this makes you credible. Speak truth gently and with compassion, without being disrespectful, and you will win hearts and minds. A big part of professionalism is lifting up others in your community. Never forget you are part of a wider network. We can pretty much guarantee that if you share, cite and credit other people's work they will return the same courtesy. So go ahead and share other posts that you agree with or from professionals you admire and respect. By doing this you are showing professional courtesy as well as providing more useful content to your followers, and not re-inventing the wheel. Winner!

3. Connection and community

When you speak to many social media experts most will tell you that a key tool to use in social media is connection. This may not be appropriate for all pages and all sizes of following, but if you have a business where developing a relationship with potential clients or customers is important then this may be a really important approach. Many potential clients want to feel they 'know' the person behind the page before making any kind of commitment. So you will need to earn their trust before they decide that you are the person they wish to learn or buy from, or whose opinion matters.

With this strategy, especially with a small page it may feel in the early days like you are 'fishing' for followers to grow your page and your business, or spread your message wider, but if you do not engage with your followers, many will move on. It's not about the number of followers but the number of meaningful interactions. To get an idea of how engaged your community is with your page, add up the number of likes, shares, and comments on a post, and divide by the number of followers you have. The bigger your page, the lower the engagement rate in general but as a rough rule, a rate of about 1-5% is considered a decent rate, although of course there will be variation between posts.

When you engage with people – they feel seen. This is essential for human relationships if you think about it. Nobody likes to feel invisible. Nobody wants to drop a comment and feel that nobody cares what they've said. Now admittedly when you have a large number of followers and get several hundred comments on a single post, it may not be possible to send each one a meaningful response, but 'liking' their comments and briefly looking through and dealing with any haters or superfans will be your main tasks.

Another aspect of building your social media that you may not necessarily see in every post or blog about building a page, is to think about the type of community you want to build. Do you want to reach a certain type of follower? How will you build inclusivity and representation in a meaningful way? How will you celebrate diversity and make people from different communities and countries feel welcome and included?

There may be many different ways of achieving this aim. One way of doing this is to create content with a global feel, using research from around the world. You can also deliberately use a huge variety of images from many different sources. Lyndsey has had people reach out and tell her that they have never seen a woman in a hijab on a meme before they found her page and it made them feel 'seen'. That's what it's all about – it's not a gimmick, but about interaction that makes a difference to people.

Of course, if you are mainly sharing evidence-based, informative content and you see your page more as an information hub, then this type of interaction with your followers may not be what you need as much as if you are trying to build a loyal following of people who will buy your products or services. Consider what you want your social media page to do for your business, and focus on the types of content, interaction and engagement that serves that purpose.

4. Types of interaction

You could also try to do joint or live events with people from different pages, promote the pages of causes you feel are important and relevant; these are also an opportunity to lift up smaller pages. This is firstly because you may be given a leg up in the early days, so pay it forward. Secondly, smaller pages have a huge amount to offer and are often sharing great content.

What about having themes, a series of posts about a particular topic, a regular day when you post about a subject, or re-post meaningful content from other pages that you trust? All of these strategies will expand your reach, meet the differing needs of your followers in varied ways, and in addition develop relationships with other creators.

Another way to engage your followers is to make community curated posts – so your followers feel useful, important and included. Asking your followers questions, doing polls, or inviting feedback and sharing the results make them feel valued. You can also share their ideas, post comments or suggestions that they send. This way if someone is struggling, many of your followers will offer support. When people feel they have a place at the table they come to eat.

Finally, value the opinions of others – this way they feel heard and respected. You can agree to disagree and you can respectfully challenge and question without being rude or aggressive. People have the right to disagree. Naturally, if they are being disrespectful, racist, homophobic or abusive in any other way, they lose the right to come and speak their mind on your page and you can - and should - delete their comments, then block them in order to protect your community. This is another way of keeping your genuine followers and fans safe. Don't feed the trolls.

5. Post regularly and reliably

People will follow pages that jump out at them while scrolling and seem to speak their language. But keeping those followers is another ballgame. To keep your followers, friends and fans interested, you need to be regular and reliable.

Firstly, be consistent – so people are reminded about you. It matters less how often you post and more about how consistently you post. Showing up in someone's feed relies on you posting regularly. There are pages that get away with ad hoc posting, but this is a risky strategy when you start out – mostly because a lot of people will lose track of time or just forget. Having a consistent and regular rhythm to your posting will help people to be reminded about you on a regular basis.

It can help to look at when your followers are most active on social media and in particular on your page, using some of the tools available on different platforms. If this time doesn't fit with your schedule you can use an app to set up scheduled posts that share to both Instagram and Facebook (more details on the practicalities of this coming up). However if you are planning any live sessions you might want to consider the best time for your audience. Often this will be in the evening around 7 - 8 pm.

Secondly, be predictable – so people know what to expect. This might mean that you always post content on a Monday, for example. You could regularly have a question and answer on a particular day, a guest feature, day-in-the-life, or share a bit of your personal life on a certain day. People like rhythms, and they will look out for your page or stories if they know to expect a certain feature. For example, people who offer a question and answer on a certain day can often expect a big increase in views of their stories on that day as people begin to expect you to show up and demonstrate that commitment to the community you are building. Also, it's an obvious point, but don't forget that your page will be growing all the time, so you will need to regularly remind people what your regular events and features are (as well as your book) so the new followers know what to expect. The followers who have been with you for a while won't mind the reminder, and may have forgotten about some of the support you offer. So don't worry about repeating yourself – just keep it brief.

6. Privacy, consent and controversy

Many people like to connect with creators and influencers who show some of their 'real' side, they are more likely to view you as authentic in the content you create and share. It's absolutely ok to share small details and be real. We would advise caution with sharing personal information, other people's information, and your children's information. Once something is on social media it can be shared, screenshots can be taken and images can be cropped or altered. So think carefully about what details you want to keep private before going ahead and posting.

With that warning over, people genuinely like to feel they 'know' the person behind the page so some judicious sharing of information, anecdote or funny stories goes a long way. Lots of people would advise caution with your religious and political views – unless this is the sole purpose of your page of course! We would personally recommend avoiding disclosing your exact whereabouts and take care not to share images that include other people or their children, who have not given express consent.

Additionally, if you are substantively employed, just be careful about the timing of your posts, or disclosing information you could only have obtained while doing your job. Social media is not worth getting fired over! Check to see if your workplace has a social media policy and only post while you are not at work. Even if you schedule your posts, you will find it distracting to get notifications or need to respond to questions while you are at work.

Finally, we would recommend having a personal social media page and a business one. You may find that you have to develop some guidelines for yourself around which friend requests you accept. Some people develop an approach of only being social media 'friends' with people they actually have a meaningful relationship with in real life. Others decide to accept nearly all friend requests but acknowledge that their social media page is almost a hybrid between a personal and professional page.

If you accept a wide range of friend requests, it's a good idea to be very careful about what you post! Unless you have a truly private page, be careful about what you post and consider who will see your status update. You may decide that you will only accept friend requests of people who have several mutual friends. One advantage of widely accepting friends is that sometimes people reach out to enquire about your book, products, or to engage you as a speaker via social media - so think carefully about how you want your page to work for you.

7. Provide helpful and valuable content

Of course, one of the main reasons people will search for, browse and stay on your page is because you generate content that is helpful and valuable to them. There are many different types of content you could consider sharing, but we'll share four main types. You should definitely consider having a combination of these types of content on your page to keep a variety of followers with different needs interested and engaged. Otherwise you run the risk of them leaving.

First of all, there are the typical 'How-to' posts. These give people practical help with something. These how-to posts may share a cunning idea, solve a problem or provide a path to a solution. They are almost always positive, and if they are aligned with the core ethos of your page (and therefore your followers' needs) they will get a lot of engagement and probably new followers too. People tend to share these a lot as they often generate a bit of a Eureka! factor. Just be careful you don't give it *all* away with these posts.

Another type of post you may want to include could be loosely grouped under the category of reassurance. These types of posts give people emotional help, are validating and kind and may offer encouragement. These posts may not get as many shares and new followers as the how-to's but they tend to be deeply appreciated by your already-loyal fans and followers. Everyone needs a post that makes them feel good about themselves from time to time. You can also share other people's posts along these lines to your stories if you'd rather stick to different types of content.

The third type of content post you could be sharing is myth busting or educational – these may deal with people's frustration and pain points.

Depending on your focus, you may be challenging bad science, common myths and misconceptions, the mainstream narrative, or providing education and information relating to practice. You may also make your challenging and educational posts part of your cause. A lot of people share these posts as they are an easy way of backing up their own viewpoints when they are struggling to make themselves heard or understood. Perhaps it's a bit passive-aggressive to send a post written by an 'expert' but many people use them as a kind of 'see, I'm not the only one' back up.

And finally, you might (if appropriate for your vibe), choose to include some light-hearted or funny content. This is where some of your personality can shine through and you show your less serious side. Most people enjoy some light relief from time to time and though this will not appeal to everyone or be the primary reason they are on your page, it will likely widen your audience.

In practice, we believe that the balance of the how-to's, reassurance, challenging and funny/light-hearted posts will be what effectively dictates the vibe of your page. If you lean more towards the myth-busting and challenging posts, your page might have a more powerful, authoritative feel, but it might also feel more argumentative or divisive. This can actually be a good way of sending a clear message about what you stand for, as people who don't like it will leave and you will be left with people who are very much aligned to your values. However, it can also generate a lot of heated debate and discussion, so be ready with your thick skin! On the other hand, if you lean more towards reassurance and normalising you are less likely to provoke arguments, but you may also find that people are looking for something more decisive and value you taking that stance.

8. Allocating appropriate amounts of time

Social media can easily take up hours of your time. It's easy to get sucked into spending much of your time scrolling, interacting, responding, posting, sharing and creating content. You may want to consider what your purpose is when you use social media. Are you trying to raise your profile to sell your book or draw traffic to your website? Are you trying to become a known authority on a topic? Or are you looking to actively attract clients?

You do need to be mindful not to invest vast amounts of time if the return you expect from social media will be small – otherwise it's simply not a good use of time and energy. Many large accounts we know consider their social media content an act of community service! Of course it's great to spread good information, but be sure you allocate it an amount of time commensurate with the income impact you expect it to generate. Whether 100% or 1% of your income is generated via social media, it makes sense to ringfence time, make yourself efficient and have a plan that you stick to make social media work for you.

9. Planning content

You could plan out your content in advance. Lyndsey produces three to four months' worth of social media content at a time. Depending on workload, if you choose this option you could either spend an entire week doing nothing but social media content writing every three months. You could also plan six months ahead, and have a rolling word document that you keep adding to. Your first step is deciding on 45-60 post titles, spreading out the how-to, reassurance, and myth busting content evenly to keep the content flow dynamic. You might think of a good post title while walking the dog or on a long car drive. Try to come up with variable length posts – sometimes they might be very short, merely asking your community a question, whereas other times they might hit the maximum character limit (depending on which social media platform you are using).

Once you have your titles written down you can simply make your way through the posts populating them. Try setting yourself a target of writing ten social media posts per week. This way, all your social media for the next period will be complete within about six weeks, but will not take you more than a couple of hours per week. One top tip here is to scan the calendar for the next few months and see if there are any major days / weeks or events coming up. For example it might be 'world day' for your specialist subject or a celebration such as Valentine's day might be coming up. It can help to align your post for that day with those events as it can help it gain more traction. Don't forget World Book Day - this, in our experience, is a great day to announce a flash sale of your book and also to ask for reviews. Remember to use this day to lift up other authors and writers!

If you prefer a more spontaneous approach that's fine. Being spontaneous allows you to catch the vibe of the moment, respond to topical issues or be flexible. Just remember to keep posting, as consistency is key. The main risk with ad hoc posting is that you might forget or be inconsistent. The other problem with it is it creates a daily or weekly 'task' that can feel heavy and burdensome. Different approaches work for different people though – perhaps experiment and see which approach you prefer. In reality you might end up with a mixed approach, planning lots of content ahead but then reacting with some spontaneous posts in reaction to current news and events.

Practical social media tips

There are entire books you can buy that are dedicated to how to create social media posts but we have put together some of the most common questions we receive below. These range from the absolute beginner to the more serious:

1. Know the 'rules' for your different platforms

If you've not had much experience of using different platforms, it's worth reading up on the different posting criteria. For example, on Instagram and TikTok you will need to create an image or video to share. You are able to post text alongside this but cannot post without the image. On Instagram you can share up to ten images per post. Conversely on Facebook and Twitter you won't need an image but they can help in attracting attention to your post. More on creating images later.

Different platforms have different character limits per post. This can be very frustrating and learning to edit is a skill in itself. On Instagram you can get around this by using images that contain text (but make sure the font is large enough to read). On Twitter you can now post linked tweets, creating your own Twitter thread. It can help to alert people to this by telling them in the first tweet that there are subtweets. A common way to do this is to number the tweets.

Finally, frustratingly, on Instagram, you cannot hyperlink blogs, articles or websites, though on Facebook this is not the case. The only way to do this on Instagram is to add a link to your posts. Previously, you had to either have a verified account, have more than 10k followers, or have a sponsored post to be able to add this feature, but recently

Instagram changed this. Links replace swipe ups, and are really useful to add an instant link to Amazon, your website, a landing page or even to share a useful article or blog.

If you don't want to add links to your stories but want to be able to get followers to your website, blogs or articles, the best way to do this on Instagram is to have your one allowed link in your bio. If you need to be able to have more than one, you can get around the problem by making your one link a landing page, or linktree where people can click to navigate to several pages. Oh, if you want to add a link on Twitter you can but might be hampered by character limits - one tip is to go to www.bitly.com and get a shortened link.

2. Understand your audiences on different platforms

Although you might think that different social media platforms are all variations on one big marketing approach, there are often important differences between who spends time on different platforms. You might find that you have loyal followers who will follow you across different platforms, but often there are subtle differences in follower demographics (i.e. age and sex) and preferred tone. As a general rule Instagram is often considered the 'friendliest' and most laid-back platform whereas Twitter can get a bit argumentative and critical. Often the exact same post will have very different reactions depending on where it is posted!

Although you can share posts using software across platforms (more details coming up on how to do that), you might find you need to tweak them slightly to your audience. You will learn the characteristics and preferences of your audience over time but each platform will have information about your followers in the settings section.

Remember that you don't have to be on every single social media platform. Decide on a primary social media platform based on what is best for your area of expertise and invest in it. Linked In may be better for some people, Clubhouse for others. Twitter may be your preferred way of networking, or you may like making TikTok videos (Hats off to you if you do!). The key is to understand your audience and be on the platform where those people are likely to hang out. Once you figure that out, invest time in working out how to get the most from your chosen social media platform. They all have their own vagaries, foibles, pros and cons, so do your research if only to protect your valuable time.

3. Consider using software or features on social media to schedule your posts

You can schedule your content using scheduling software such as Hootsuite, Later or Sprout. You can also use Meta Business Suite to compose posts on Facebook and Instagram and schedule them to be posted at a time that seems to be a popular engagement time for your followers. On Facebook you can only currently do this on a page you manage, not your personal page. You can share the same post to Facebook and Instagram using this tool, although you might want to edit your post depending on your followers on each platform.

To do this via Facebook:

- Go to your page
- Go to 'Manage Page'
- Click on 'Publishing tools'
- Click on 'Create post'
- Either write it out there and then, including any images or gifs, or copy and paste your post from a document you prepared earlier
- Click on 'share now' and select 'schedule'
- Select the time and date, and click 'schedule' - and you're done.

There are also software packages you can use to do this for you, and these work in much the same way but with a few advantages:

- You can schedule content to more platforms with software such as Hootsuite, whereas the scheduling functions on Instagram and Facebook only allow you to schedule content to those platforms. This may be all you need but if you want to post to LinkedIn, Twitter and YouTube, then you might find utilising software more helpful.

- Many scheduling tools select or suggest the best engagement times for your page and will help you release the content at a time that will benefit your business. This is likely to help with the reach and performance of your post.

- Most scheduling tools have better integration with other software such as Canva and allow access to gifs and stock images which is helpful if you need a wide selection of images.

With any scheduling tool, you can pause scheduled posts to be respectful of a crisis or unexpected emergency that arises where your scheduled content would be inappropriate or out of place. Keeping an eye on your scheduled posts is a good plan to avoid a massive faux pas.

Another tool you might find useful is a social media content calendar. Some of the special days are really obscure and may not be appropriate to your target audience. Remember, you don't have to appeal to everyone. If National Welly Throwing day doesn't fit with the vibe of your page, you don't have to try to fit your content around dates that feel irrelevant. But content calendars can be an excellent way to ensure you don't forget major religious festivals, anniversaries, or special dates relevant to your specialty.

4. Use hashtags to increase visibility of your posts

Hashtags work to 'file' your post in the right 'directory'. It's a bit like an old-fashioned phone book. If you were looking for a plumber in a phone book or on Google, you'd search for 'plumber', or possibly 'plumber in London' if you wanted to narrow the search. Hashtags essentially do the same thing. Some people follow certain hashtags, and using them means your posts will get found by those searching for content on that topic who previously had not come across your work.

You can also create community by using hashtags – such as #AuthorsOfInstagram; or find local colleagues who use location specific hashtags – such as #DevonDoula, or #LifeCoachNewYork. One top piece of advice is to capitalise the first letter of new words in the hashtags, as this makes it more accessible for those who rely on screen readers and other assistive technology. On a similar note, adding subtitles to videos and describing the image is a good way of increasing accessibility.

Do not make all your hashtags the same, but at the same time have a fair amount of crossover. Instagram frequently issues guidance about the 'right' number or the 'right' way to use hashtags – have a look at their suggestions, as they vary. In the last year or so, they have fluctuated between recommending 15-20 hashtags, and then just five to six, so you'll need to check.

One final warning – do not use 'banned' hashtags. These will mean that nobody can find your post because other users have reported them for violation of the guidelines. They're not always the most obvious ones either so this is worth a Google as they may change from time to time.

Examples of banned hashtags include #HumpDay, #adulting, #brain, #killingit and so on.

Finally, although you can use hashtags across platforms, they are less useful on Facebook than they are on Instagram. Consider removing them from Facebook posts as sometimes they can irritate followers and on Twitter you will probably find that they take up too many characters.

5. Use the 'stories' feature on Facebook and Instagram

Don't forget about your stories. Many followers (particularly on Instagram) don't look through someone's grid, or keep on scrolling. They just go straight to their stories and flick through. Stories only remain visible for 24 hours so to keep your story (and therefore your message) at the top of someone's feed, you'll need to regularly post to stories. The good news is that this is a *lot* quicker than creating content. Some people post content to their grid very infrequently, but compensate by having very active stories. There is now a feature on Instagram that allows you to share your stories to the stories of a linked Facebook account.

On Instagram you can engage with your community using stories – try polls, question boxes, votes and invite responses. You can also tag other people and share other respected accounts' posts to your stories. Stories take seconds and they are well worth keeping active.

6. Set yourself boundaries for how much time you will spend on social media

One practical tip is to decide how much time you want to spend on social media and stick to it. It's important to have boundaries. Many people find it helpful to plan out a rough timetable of activity so they don't end up getting sucked in. When Lyndsey runs a question and answer box she typically gets thousands of questions. This could easily be overwhelming but accepting that all you can ever do is answer a sample of them will release you from this burden. Here are some ideas for how to set boundaries:

- Try setting yourself a one-hour time limit and when the hour is up - no more questions. You may decide an hour is too much.
- Some people have a social media day per week where they work on content, design memes, and so on.
- Others have a time of day when they do all their social media.

Find the rhythm that works for you and protect your social media free time. We'd also encourage you to be protective of a social media free day per week – this is a great act of self-care.

7. Choose your images carefully

Most people appreciate an image to accompany your written content, so you can source your images and attach these to your captions. On Facebook or Twitter, it matters a lot less how your images look next to each other, as people won't see all your posts together when they scroll. On Instagram, many social media experts say that it does matter a bit more what your grid looks like. Here are some ideas of different ways you can plan to set out your grid on Instagram to look visually appealing:

- Some people post alternating logo and image sequences to create a chequerboard.
- Other people have a personalised colour scheme they stick to or you might choose black and white images only.
- Some people have fairly random images but always consistently use their brand logo in the corner - this helps people to identify the work as yours, in case it is shared or reposted.
- You could have regular themed content with its own distinctly different visual appearance to highlight to your followers what the post is about.
- Conversely, you might go for the brightest and most colourful images you can find, or alternate between grayscale and colour.
- You could go for the random approach, where you allow your personality to speak the loudest, and not worry too much about what your grid looks like overall.

Thinking about the layout of your grid on a platform like Pinterest or Instagram which are both very visual platforms might feel like a headache, but equally this may feel like the fun part if you are creatively minded. Remember to do what works best for you and the time and headspace you have available.

Above all though, think about the quality of your image. Choose images that are high resolution, royalty free, or images that you have paid for via a subscription or download rights. The image should also clearly depict visually what you are trying to convey. You will always get some people who argue with you about your choice of image, so spend some time carefully considering your images to avoid people pointing out a factual inaccuracy.

8. Link to other pages and experts

When you create posts and content, it can be really helpful to link to other pages. This is especially relevant if you are referring to a subject that is not your direct specialism, or want to credit the work of another professional or page. Pointing people in the direction of relevant other pages by saying something like; 'Make sure you head over to @BrilliantSocialMedia page for more tips' means that you are doing several things well. Firstly, you're staying in your scope of practice. Secondly, you're lifting up another page, networking and building trusting connections. Thirdly, you're adding value to your community by providing a trusted source where they can go to get more help. Referring to and citing other pages is a great way to be authentic, credible and behave with integrity.

9. Consider hiring an expert

If all this sounds overwhelming then we'll leave you with one final cheat - you can hire social media experts, virtual assistants and graphic designers to take a lot of the pain out of social media. This may not feel like a cost-effective idea initially but if you find that social media is a successful way of generating clients, it may get to a point where it works in your favour to outsource. You can find numerous freelancers on sites such as People Per Hour, or Fiverr, or consider hiring a social media manager. Asking colleagues and friends for personal recommendations is often a good way to ensure that you find someone who fits your ethos and with whom you gel.

Chapter 15

Giving presentations

If you have read this book in order and only just got your head around talking to the occasional journalist you might start off this chapter thinking, 'wait - there's more?'. Don't panic. First of all, you do not actually have to give a presentation or speak at a conference if you don't want to. If the mere thought of speaking in public, to actual people who might have (horror of horrors) paid to be there, gives you hives you could just skip this section. Your secret is safe with us. If you are even remotely open-minded about the idea though, stick around while we try to persuade you that presenting your work is a good idea.

Publishing a book, or writing an academic article for that matter, frequently presents an opportunity to speak or present. It is often inevitable that you will be asked to speak - although this can depend on your subject matter and how competitive and crowded your particular field is. Once your work is published and in the public eye it makes you easier to find. Those searching for a presenter on a particular topic will often look to newly published authors, and speaking circuits are always on the look-out for fresh speakers. After all, you probably wouldn't go to a conference if you had heard all the speakers and the same talks before. So there is actually an ongoing need for new faces.

Writing a book usually demonstrates considerable knowledge in your field. Who therefore, is better suited to give a presentation on your subject? It is assumed that if you have written a book you probably know a thing or two, and not only that but you can explain it well.

We totally understand that writing a book, burying yourself in research articles, and tapping away on your laptop are entirely different tasks to standing up on a podium in front of people and speaking. Perhaps when you started writing your book you never even considered that you would be asked to *talk* about it? Perhaps you have some lingering impostor syndrome or a negative seed of doubt that nobody would want to listen to you. Square your shoulders, lift your head up and go back a few chapters to read about overcoming impostor syndrome. You just wrote a book. If people want to buy it, they will definitely want to hear you talk about it. Trust us.

Presenting your work at conferences, study days and other opportunities is a good thing for a number of reasons:

Firstly, it will be good publicity. Not everyone who hears you speak will have bought your book. Some people might be waiting to hear you speak before they decide whether or not to buy your book and read more of what you have to say: Think of it like a commercial for your book. Presenting may remind people who had vaguely heard about you or your work and keep your book on their radar. Some people might have bought your book but it has been added to the ever-growing pile of books to read. Hearing you speak might make them want to pick it up. This is obviously a good thing. When you wrote the book, you didn't just want people to buy it, but read it as well.

Speaking publicly gives your book a wider audience. You may reach people who have never heard of it, particularly if you speak in a different country to the one where your book was published. You may also have an opportunity to 'sell' your book to cynics and sceptics. Perhaps those who need persuading will be won over by your charm and charisma... you never know.

Speaking in public is altruistic. Presumably one of your aims for your book was to spread the word about an important topic. Perhaps you wrote to educate, inform, challenge or encourage. Speaking at an event means more people hear the important message you have to give.

It may increase your credibility as you become a known authority. Presenting is an excellent way for people to find out about you, which is important if you have research and information to share. Presenting widely will increase your credibility - we're not suggesting that you'll become an overnight celebrity in your field but it's certainly a way of becoming known as an authority on a particular topic. When you consider conferences, you might check who else is speaking to help you decide whether to attend. Everyone knows that attending a conference is not just about hearing the speakers, but at the same time they are a big factor in the decision making. If your name keeps showing up on conference programmes, your status as a leader in your field is somewhat confirmed. Of course, you have to then justify and maintain this honour but we'll get to that!

It is an excellent way to network and meet people. On the subject of conferences not being just about hearing a speaker, one of the major bonuses of attending a conference, especially a face to face one, is the networking. We have lost count of the number of important and lifelong connections we have made through attending and speaking at conferences. They are wonderful for meeting like-minded people. The nature of a conference is that they tend to attract people who have similar interests and skills. This provides an amazing opportunity to gather in one place for an extended amount of time and make useful contacts. As an invited speaker this is even more the case, because people will want to talk to you and pick your brain in the breaks.

Admittedly, for introverts (like both of us for what it's worth) large crowds of people can be exhausting. Do not assume for a moment that you can't pull this out of the bag even if you too prefer your own company to the hustle and bustle of a crowded room. You may need to pencil in a day to socially recover after a conference, but on balance it's probably worth it.

It provides an opportunity for growth and development. At the risk of sounding like your senior school careers advisor, presenting at conferences and events is a great way to grow in confidence and develop new skills. This may sound cringeworthy but speaking publicly is about more than just CV points. Learning to present orally and getting better at this will stand you in good stead at many points in your career. Speaking in public forces you to be brave, clearly articulate your ideas and showcase your work. You will have to distil your thinking and the main ideas from your book, or paper, into a talk that holds your audience's attention (and fits within a prescribed time slot!). These are great skills that will add to your poise and confidence.

Writing and giving presentations helps you develop areas for future work and writing. As you create presentations, you will be forced to brush up your knowledge, scour the literature for new and updated material and read around. These activities in themselves will make you more expert in your field. Particularly if you are invited to speak at more than one event you will have to develop a range of presentations, otherwise you will be the proverbial one-trick-pony. In order to generate new material, you will have to consider fresh topics or go even deeper into your specialism.

Getting your first invitation to speak

You've published your book, anxiously awaited the first few reviews and then the email inviting you to speak at a conference lands in your inbox. How you might feel and how you respond are fairly individual. If you're busy and stressed, it's likely this invitation brings mixed feelings. If you're longing to 'get out there' you may feel wildly excited immediately followed by crushing anxiety. There are also times you feel it is right to say no. For professionals in certain fields, it is unwise to speak at conferences that have received sponsorship from a company that is considered unethical in your field. You may need to do some digging about this depending on your exact profession.

You may be wondering, if you have been invited to speak on the strength of your book, how much crossover material you will cover in a presentation. It's important, obviously, not to simply regurgitate the book. The conference organisers and audience want to hear you speak about this subject but there has to be added value compared to them simply reading the book. How do you not just repeat the book?

Well, remember that not everyone will have read your book and even if they have they won't remember all of the content. So don't panic that your talk needs to be entirely unique. Often, people appreciate the highlight reel version of your book to bring it to life. Think about:

- Linking your work with practical examples
- Telling stories to make your theory come to life
- Share key tips, takeaways and provide a succinct summary
- Highlight the key evidence-based messages
- Making it topical - if there happens to be a current issue that your book is related to, this can work well

One of the next questions you might have is how much to charge for speaking. There are many variables to bear in mind when you think about this. First of all, inexperienced speakers normally command smaller fees. Well-known speakers can often justify a bigger fee because a 'big name' will draw a big crowd and conference organisers know they can shift tickets if their keynote is a famous or sought-after speaker - which makes it financially worth their while.

A major factor influencing the speaker budget is the conference organiser, their resources, the overheads of running the event and whether there is any sponsorship. Having organised and been involved with many events, it is remarkably common for expenses to run away. Conference organisers on a small budget often try to sweeten the deal of a small speaker fee with free conference attendance, free vendor stalls or a speaker dinner. On the other hand, for established events where large audiences can be guaranteed, there may be a bigger budget. Online events may have a bigger budget as they have fewer overheads in terms of venue hire, hotel conferencing and catering costs, though they will have digital, technical and marketing costs.

Some events may attract sponsorship. This is not always unethical, but it's a good idea to check who the sponsors are in case they do not align with your ethos or put you in an embarrassing position. For example, if your talk is all about reusable cloth nappies at a baby conference and the major sponsor is a disposable nappy company, you may feel like this is too big a conflict of interest. Often though, the sponsors may be small businesses who sponsor the event in order to get exposure to an invested audience. Conference organisers also generate revenue by having vendor stalls or marketplaces, where exhibitors sell their products. All this increases the potential budget.

Some conferences that we have spoken at have a policy of not paying their speakers at all. They will pay for expenses such as a hotel room, and some travel reimbursement, plus a speaker dinner event, but no speaker fee. However, if you are submitting to an academic conference, always double check that they will reimburse these costs. In the very different world of academia most speakers do not get reimbursed, and often on top of that still have to pay the full conference fee themselves as well.

Sometimes speaking for free is worth it, because the event may give you a lot of exposure. It might mean that you get to attend for free when you usually wouldn't have the budget. It might lead to bigger opportunities to speak and more book sales. You might meet new people and make new connections. You might just really like the city it is in or desperately want a weekend away, leaving your children behind. Every conference and opportunity is different and we will have to leave it to you to decide whether the effort, time and hassle of going away is worth it. It's a very individual decision and depends to a great extent on what you perceive you will be likely to accomplish by speaking, who you may meet, or whether it is important to be seen as an authority by the people you want to network with.

If you are ever asked by a conference or event organiser what your speaker fee is, consider:

- How long it will take you to write your presentation. Some presentations can be developed quickly or adapted. However, brand new material takes time to develop into a rock-solid presentation. We would usually allow at least two weeks to write a brand-new presentation, including the time it takes to perform a literature search, summarise the evidence, refine the objectives and then create the slides.

- Whether you need to allow time to practice and edit your presentation. If you are not experienced at teaching or presenting, you may need to allow time to make sure you can present your work in the time allowed and that your material flows logically. This gets easier with practice but in the beginning you may need to be generous with your timescales to yourself.

- Whether you have any associated costs - such as buying images for your presentation. Many images can be sourced for free, from sources like Canva, Unsplash, Burst, Pexels and Stocksnap. However, sometimes the perfect image has to be bought from sites such as Shutterstock. It can work out to be quite expensive to buy photos and images.

- Where the conference is and how long you will be away. This can require some juggling of other commitments, coordination with a partner or your work. The hassle factor is not insignificant.

- Will you have any additional childcare costs or pet care costs while you are away? Think about the time, hassle and cost of asking friends and family (down to the thank you gift you may need to buy), booking childcare, babysitters, dog walkers and pet sitters.

- Your travel costs. Think about all your travel costs, including:
    - Petrol and wear and tear on your car
    - Car parking at a venue or airport
    - Flights, taxes, and luggage costs
    - Travel to / from your hotel to the venue - car rental or taxis
    - Any meals that you will be expected to fund while away

    - The cost of socialising - many excellent connections are made at the bar or after-party
    - Loss of income if you have to take time off work to speak
    - Buying an outfit if you usually live in leggings / sweats!

- Whether you would be able to recycle or amend this presentation for another audience. Some conferences insist on an original talk for copyright reasons. This limits how much you can spread the cost of creating this presentation as you would not be able to deliver it in the same format again.

- How much your time is worth, in terms of being away from home and family. Being away from home can be hard work. While it sounds glamorous to be in hotels and dining out, the reality is that it can be tiring, lonely, overwhelming and stressful. Not everyone sleeps well if they are not in their own bed, or you may have health or dietary challenges that make going away additionally stressful. What is all *that* hassle worth?

- How much you want to speak at the conference and whether there will be additional benefits and opportunities to you. Sometimes it is an amazing opportunity that you feel you can't pass up for professional credibility and exposure reasons.

- Whether there are opportunities to sell your book at the event and whether the audience are likely to be interested in that. Not all conferences provide opportunity to sell your book or you may be expected to pay for a stall. Some events may not even allow you to plug your book. It's worth checking, as this may be a significant factor in your decision making.

- Whether you will lose income indirectly by providing information to an audience who may be essentially your competitors.

- What other speakers in your field charge. They may make this publicly available information. Try looking on the websites of people in your field to find their speaker fee or ask around. Remember however that if they have more experience than you, or draw in a bigger audience then they may be able to charge more. Based on this you may want to adjust your fee as you become more experienced.

Having said all of that, you may wish to have a sliding scale, so that charities and companies providing education to under-represented or low-income groups can benefit from your knowledge. Sometimes it pays to be altruistic. We have both spoken for free or highly subsidised rates for charities with tiny budgets where they are providing the tickets free of charge, or donating ticket sales to access funds, and so on. You could consider having a commercial rate and a charity rate for organisers who are either not charging for tickets or have no sponsorship.

Finally, not all conferences actually invite speakers. Some conferences have a system where there is a window of time to allow potential speakers to submit an abstract. The advantage of this is that there are no surprises and you get to have a lot of control over what you offer to speak about - and to whom. Some of these conferences are less likely to pay - especially major professional organisations but they are also more likely to have large audiences and therefore be a good opportunity to present your work to a highly relevant audience.

Sometimes these conferences have a mixture of invited keynote speakers, as well as a selection committee who review the talk proposals. The abstract submission process often allows you to say what your fees and expenses are as well as making your AV (audio-visual) requests. One advantage of the abstract submission system is that this often allows for speakers from under-represented groups to be given an opportunity, increases the variety of speakers and topics and can also raise the standard of presentations.

If you decide to submit a talk abstract, this is not unlike a book proposal in terms of how you prepare it, though thankfully it is much shorter. You will need to carefully consider the audience, and therefore what is likely to appeal to the abstract selection panel. You will need to consider your topic, the key objectives of your talk and why the audience needs to hear this material. You will also probably be required to provide some up to date references for your talk.

Think of the abstract as essentially your elevator pitch: how you would describe the importance of what you are proposing to talk about in the 30 seconds it takes to ride in an elevator from the ground floor to the 10th. Imagine you only have that long to convince the person next to you of how important your topic is. If you cannot distil your message into something that takes 30 seconds to explain, keep working on it. It really is worth being able to succinctly share your message.

Unless you are a globally renowned expert on your subject with a reputation that goes before you, you will probably from time to time be trying to persuade someone who has not heard of you that you should speak. Imagine that someone outside your field and area of expertise is reviewing abstracts. They know nothing about your subject. You have the length of your abstract, which might be 300-500 words, to convince them that your talk is important, topical and interesting.

Therefore when you are writing your abstract make sure that you write clearly and concisely, articulating what the problem is and how you will attempt to solve it or make sense of it. The key is to keep it simple and not try to cover too many things. You can expand on the themes in your talk but the abstract is really just to hook people in. The conference organisers will probably use your abstract in their publicity materials, so think of it as your chance to convince people to listen to you. Essentially it is the conference equivalent of the blurb on the back of your book. Just as people judge books by their covers, they judge talks and speakers by their abstracts.

Distilling your work into a short presentation

Once you have wrapped your head around needing to stand up and give a presentation, you'll probably turn your attention to writing the slides. Not all presentations require a slide deck; for example, some TED talks have no slides, or just one or two powerful images or quotes. However, this type of talk requires exceptional oral presentation skills and can feel very intimidating. The exception is when you are telling a powerful story. If the story in itself is profound, then slides may be considered superfluous - but be careful, as this can leave you feeling rather exposed.

For many presenters, having a slide deck (known as a PowerPoint presentation in old terms!) provides a structure to your talk and allows you to get your audience from the starting point to the conclusion in the way that you want. Your talk should provide a logical roadmap, it helps to think about it in the same way that you think about the macro structure of your book. Work out your objectives and think about the chain of arguments or points you need to make in order to reach your conclusion and achieve those objectives on the way.

Also remember that your presentation should help your audience make sense of what you are saying. You do not want them to be spending the time looking at your slides - ideally these should just be a reminder, and not distract your audience from what you are saying. To keep it simple, your presentation will probably broadly have the following macro-structure:

Introducing yourself: This is probably the section that can run away in terms of time, so keep this brief. You'll need to form a rapport with your audience, so this is a good place to share one or two personal details that you don't mind being public, as it can make you more relatable. Humour is also a good tool at this point - it breaks the ice, and will help you to relax. An alternative is to start with something powerful that grips your audience from the very start. Only you know which approach is more likely to go down well. Aim for just 2-3 minutes on this, or you'll run out of time for the content - which is obviously the most important part.

Disclosure statement: Although this is a very short part of your talk, it does need to be specifically mentioned. Many conference organisers will expect to see a disclosure statement where you can declare any research affiliations, funding, positions of responsibility that could influence your position, royalties or sponsorships. This is to ensure transparency and honesty to your audience. Many people also use this time to acknowledge sources of help, someone who was instrumental, or their privilege. In some countries it is also appropriate to acknowledge the indigenous people on whose lands you now speak.

Privacy and consent to share: You will also want to be clear about whether you mind people taking photos of your slides as you speak. Many presenters don't mind photos for personal use, but the problem is that some people will share these to their social media. If you do not have permission for a certain photo, or unpublished data to be shared liberally on Twitter, make it clear what your audience can and cannot do before you start your talk.

Aims and objectives: This is the section where you tell your audience what they can expect the session to encompass. For a lot of conferences, this is how they get the session accredited for continuing professional development. Essentially, they usually require 3-5 learning objectives that are specific and measurable. For example, a good learning objective would be: 'At the end of this presentation, learners will know the 3 most common causes of headache'. A poor learning objective would be: 'At the end of this presentation, learners will understand headaches'. This second example is non-specific, the result being that it is more difficult for someone to reflect on the session and confirm that they do in fact, understand headaches better.

Problem statement: It's often a good idea to contextualise your talk, giving the importance and rationale for why this topic is important. For example, you might lead with some current research into the impact of headaches on quality of life, daily functioning and productivity. You could then explain how you are planning to address this problem in your talk. This isn't just a re-statement of your aims and objectives, but really making it practical and relevant to your audience.

Content: Clearly this section should make up the bulk of your talk. You will have a selection of slides covering your main argument, research findings, or practical suggestions. Conventional wisdom is to think about having approximately 1 slide per minute. There are times when this is not appropriate, such as when you are reviewing data from a research study, and talking through the results of a paper. But on the whole, think about your audience sitting still. They often like to have an interesting slide to look at and hold their attention. This is perhaps even more important when you are delivering an online talk. If an occasional slide requires you to spend more time on it, that's fine, but if every slide takes 5 minutes, you may find people start to shift in their seats, unless you are telling a particularly engaging story.

There are problems with the one slide per minute rule. One is that if you run over, you can quickly end up with a massively overrunning presentation, or needing to skip several slides at the end in a panic to finish. Another is that obviously this takes more time to create, and needs more images or non-written content to make the presentation attractive. We generally find that about 45 slides for a 1-hour talk is about right, because although some slides will be brief, we know we tend to hover on certain sections, and we want to allow time to ad lib, react to the audience, or be spontaneous.

Summary: You will have covered your objectives in the body of your talk, but in the summary section, you will remind your audience what they have learned. So if your objective was that they would know the 3 most common causes of headache - this is the part where you remind them what the 3 most common causes are. The summary is where you bring it all together - do not be tempted to use this section to introduce a brand-new concept.

Questions: Always allow time for questions - even if you have rendered the audience speechless, and there is a bonus ten minutes at the end, nobody will mind. When you liaise with the conference organisers, you will find out how long they want you to talk for. We've learned that some organisers request a 1-hour talk with Q & A afterwards, while others expect time for questions to be allowed within your 1-hour talk. For goodness sake find out which - or you may either feel rushed, or run out of time and get mobbed by all the folks who didn't have a chance to ask their burning question.

Closing and contact details: It's a good idea to have a final slide with a thank you, your social media handles, website and email address.

Practice makes perfect

We cannot stress enough the importance of practising your presentation, especially if you are new to presenting. There may come a time when you know your material and your subject so well you can pretty much stand up and eloquently talk off the cuff. However, at the beginning most people need to practise. Knowing your presentation on 'paper' so to speak, and knowing what it feels like to present, are two very different things. If you don't rehearse it, you may get to a slide and have the sense that you've never seen your presentation before in your life, despite having spent days polishing it.

Practising your presentation is important because it helps you learn how to talk around the slide, and work out whether the order that made sense to you on paper, actually makes sense when you deliver it verbally. The best presentations are when the presenter is obviously familiar with their work, understands it completely, talks around the content of the slide, and is able to refer to it without reading it verbatim (with the exception of specific quotes).

Think about your transitions. No, we don't mean those really irritating features in PowerPoint where words fly in or make a clicking noise - this is commonly referred to as 'death by PowerPoint'. We mean how you get from one slide to the next. When you polish and rehearse your presentation, think about what you will say so that your content flows. This is why rehearsing is so important. Sometimes, it is only during a practice that you realise the transition from one slide to another feels clunky, or you've missed a logical link. As you rehearse, note down the transitions that don't feel right, or where you think you may be repeating yourself, or missing a step.

After you've rehearsed your talk, go back and edit the sections you weren't happy with. This includes spreading content out over more slides if you find you hover for a disproportionately long time on one slide compared to others. You may also find that you need to develop more succinct ways of saying things if you find yourself over-running. Some conferences are very strict with time keeping, and if there is very little leeway, you may want to consider either noting down the time you should be moving on to the next slide in the 'notes' section of your presentation or using a stopwatch / timer.

Tips for formatting and style

What your presentation looks like is important. If it's good, people will remember the presentation as a whole. If it needs work, what may happen is that the audience can't quite connect with your talk. It's the old adage that people often only notice something if it's bad. Remember, you are the main tool of your presentation, not the presentation itself. The slide deck should support what you say, not detract from it. Presentations vary considerably, but here are some general tips for developing your presentation:

- Avoid numerous bullet points on one slide, especially on a white background. If you have several points to make, spread them out over a few slides - it will keep the slides moving, and hold your audience's attention better. It certainly seems ironic that this tip appears in a bullet-pointed list, and personally we think bullet points are really useful for splitting up a longer point you're making. Just don't over-do them on a slide.

- For a pre-recorded presentation that can be paused and rewound, you can get away with more writing on a slide. However, if you are delivering live, you don't want your audience to be torn between reading your slides and listening to you.

- If you have lots of data or information to share, consider making a handout for your audience so they can refer to their conference materials to get this, without it cluttering up your slides.
- Use images to tell stories and augment your words. Make sure your images are pertinent and high quality, not blurry.
- Keep your language relevant to your audience - patronising a highly learned audience, or pitching it too high for a wider audience are both no-nos.
- If you use abbreviations, make sure you explain them. Abbreviations can be annoying to an audience because even if you explain the first time, people may forget, particularly if it is an abbreviation that is uncommon or unfamiliar.
- Keep the font size large - between 24-32 often works well. Some conferences may specify a minimum size if the room is very large.
- Be careful about the colours of your background and your font. You need to consider accessibility - some people find certain colours really difficult to see, especially if they have dyslexia. Making your font yellow is almost never a good idea!
- Avoid overly themed templates - these can limit the number of people who find your presentation relevant. A happy medium is what we're after.
- Consider having your brand colour as a subtle accent, and include a small logo if you like. It's also a good idea to put Your Name © at the bottom of the slide, to remind less scrupulous members of the audience that this is your intellectual property, and just because they paid to hear you speak at a conference, does not mean they can re-package this talk as their own. You can add a watermark, and any handout you produce can also have a watermark, or be given in PDF format to make it harder to copy.
- Use a clear font, like Arial or Calibri, and avoid novelty fonts. Check with the conference organisers because some of them insist on a branded template with a specific font.

In terms of what to put on your slides besides writing, you have numerous options, depending a little on your topic, and the audience. Tools you could incorporate into your presentation to keep the audience engaged include:

Pictures: The picture you choose may be metaphorical, suggestive, or illustrate your point. There are so many places where you can source high quality images that it should be no problem finding one that fits the bill. Sometimes, you can make a powerful visual impact by using only a picture. This can also be a way of limiting the chance of plagiarism as well. After all, nobody will be able to deliver the line the way you can. This does rely on you being able to talk without any written prompts, however, and works best when you know your subject inside out, and know you can stick to the time available.

Analogies and stories: You may wish to tell a figurative story to illustrate your point. Analogies and stories that you know really well can often be a great way to connect with your audience, be relatable, and also help you to relax. You could just have a key phrase on the slide to prompt you, and remind your audience what your main point is, but this allows you the opportunity to speak freely.

Humour and anecdote: There is definitely a time and a place for humour and anecdote. A formal, serious conference full of serious people there to learn is possibly not the time for a knock-knock joke. However, it is a universal truth that people like to laugh, and be entertained. It's a tricky balance though, because if you're not a natural comedian this can feel forced and cringeworthy. If you are keen to use humour, a less scary option than telling a joke is to tell a story or anecdote that you know well, and know to be funny.

Charts and graphs: Visually representing a poll, or some data that is interesting can sometimes come across better with a chart or graph than endless numbers or description. A pie chart that clearly illustrates a proportion or an amount may visually deliver the impact you want much more effectively.

Statistics: These can be a really powerful way to make or prove a point. Lyndsey often says that she hates statistics, but specifically what she dislikes is figuring out what statistical tests to use. Statistics - even if you loathe maths - are a great way to succinctly summarise the state of a situation. Love them or hate them, we all use stats in everyday life. They quickly help us to contextualise how prevalent or meaningful something is, and speak for themselves.

Case studies: These are subtly different from stories, and can be a really good way to get some audience interaction as well. Case studies are often a scenario that you present. You can reveal some of the case study, and then depending on the size of the audience, you could invite people to offer their thoughts or ideas, or with larger audiences, raise their hands or vote in some way. You can then reveal more of the story, building a more complex picture. Case-based learning is particularly popular with clinicians and can help link theory to practice.

Quotes: Sometimes a quote can be very powerful. You can use these in different ways. It could be a quote from a research participant, a well-known thought leader, poet, or even a catchphrase. In fact, these are the exceptions to the 'never read out your slides' rule.

Video: If you really want to grab your audience's attention, a video might be just what you need. A really well constructed video can sometimes eloquently convey something punchy in just a minute or two and save you a lot of back story and explanation. You can also use video interviews, or videos of procedures, clinical signs, or techniques to show your audience what you mean, rather than try to explain it.

Remember, all these tools should help the audience take away something meaningful from your talk. They should not be the *most* important part. A beautifully presented slide deck should be the icing on the cake of a fantastic and memorable presentation, not the key ingredient. That job is yours, as scary as that might sound!

Polishing your presentation:

Once you have designed your slides it's worth doing some final checks and edits of your work. Some useful things to remember include:

1. Spell checking – have any errors sneaked in? Has any software or auto correct function changed how words are spelled without you realising it?

2. Formatting – are slides formatted consistently? When you look at them in sequence have you used similar sized headings, colours and font so that it looks like a consistent piece?

3. Fact checking – are you confident everything is correct? Double check references and details of research studies you have included.

4. Flow and feel – how does it feel when you practice speaking it out loud? Are your transitions between slides smoothe?

5. Time checking – make sure the timings add up correctly with a little leeway in case you speed up or give more detail on the day.

Tips for managing public speaking

It's normal for everyone to feel anxious to some degree about getting up in front of a room full of people to speak. You're putting yourself out there and it's daunting. Do not expect to ever feel entirely calm, some healthy nerves are actually a tool you can harness. Don't forget, one of the purposes of our stress response is to increase our alertness. Try to reframe the nerves as positive stress - this helps a lot. Most audiences will be generous to a speaker who has some nerves - after all, the majority of the audience wouldn't be asked to get up and speak to a room full of people, and so they tend to forgive speakers who need a drink of water, or have a nervous laugh.

If you feel like you are likely to be nervous, our advice is to really polish your introduction so you know it like the back of your hand. Most people find that if they can get through the first 2 minutes and realise that the stage isn't going to swallow them whole, they start to relax. We're not suggesting that you don't polish the rest of your talk, but really make sure the beginning is perfect.

1. Ask about who will be in your audience in advance

We would definitely recommend knowing an approximate audience size, as this may influence how you present. Speaking to a group of 25-40 may allow for some pair work, or reflection in groups. With an audience of 500, this obviously would not work in a meaningful way. Impostor syndrome will probably tell you that your nerves will be directly proportional to the audience size; but honestly, when you're standing on a stage, the lighting is often such that you can't really see them. The difference between 200 and 800 is also not worth worrying about. If you can get up and speak to 50 people, what difference do a few more make...?! What can actually be more off-putting is seeing the watch count growing on an online presentation, as sometimes these can grow to vast numbers, and fluctuate too. Another word of advice here - try not to watch the numbers, it will distract you.

2. Know your content

The golden rule is to never, ever read your slides - which you will find much easier if you have rehearsed your talk. The bullet points on your slides should serve as a summary of what you are speaking about on that slide. On a similar note, do not read cue cards, or a printed script in front of you either. Most of us have experienced presentations where the speaker did not engage with the audience, and simply read their slides, script, or notes. We guarantee, if you do this, people will be thinking the same thing: 'I could have just read the slides myself'. People want to hear what you have to say, but they do not want to be read to. A huge part of presenting is learning how to give your message in a way that tells a story, grabs your audience's attention and is entertaining for them.

Many people have some notes just in case you have a moment where everything you thought you knew seems to exit your brain. One tip is to print off your presentation in handout form and write one or two notes against each slide. Another tip is that if you lose your train of thought, repeat the last thing you said as you slowly and casually walk back to your notes for a recap. Everyone will think you're just repeating it for emphasis, we promise!

Some people learn their presentation, and this can work well for a very short talk where additional words and fluff will add considerably to the time it takes to deliver your talk. In those situations it can help to practice your presentation several times until you are certain you can deliver it in the time allowed. In general though, learning or scripting a talk that you deliver live can give it a forced feel. Of course, when you give a presentation many times you will end up repeating the same key phrases, or telling the same stories in the same way, but this is not the same as a learned monologue.

3. Don't forget to breathe

Stop and breathe - remembering to breathe through your nose, not your mouth (mouth breathing will just dry your mouth out!). Speak slowly, clearly and leave time for pauses. Don't be afraid to move your hands if this is natural for you - remember that communication is not all about what you say, but how you say it. Your non-verbal communication matters too. Your facial expressions, head movements, and even your silence, can be as powerful as your words.

4. Ask about sound options

You may not have a choice, but if you are given the option of a static microphone behind a lectern, or a roving mic or headset, consider which will make you feel more at ease. For some, particularly more anxious speakers, you may feel 'safer' behind a lectern - it places a physical barrier between you and your audience which might make you feel more secure. It also means that you won't be expected to move about - which may be what you want. However, if you prefer to walk around, using your body to make your point as you speak, then you will prefer a headset.

A microphone can be annoying to hold for any length of time and means you can't move your hands as you speak. Not only do you have to hold the microphone at just the right distance from your mouth, but also, although it doesn't weigh much, you can get a sore wrist after a while. Yes, we know that sounds pathetic, but it's true. Holding a static position for a long time is hard, and you'll end up needing to switch hands. Don't be afraid to make these AV requests of the conference organisers - they will want to keep their speakers happy after all.

If the worst happens and there is no sound system installed (or it is faulty), you will need to project. If this ever happens to you, take a glass of water, as it's harder work. You will need to keep your head up high to allow your voice to carry to the back of the room. This is another reason it is always best to check in advance what sound equipment is being used, as people with naturally quieter voices may be able to make a request if there is enough notice.

5. Think about your clothing choices

Do consider what you are wearing. Consider whether there will be any seated presentations and what might happen to skirt length (there is more on this in Chapter 16, coming up next). Will you feel more confident blending in by wearing black or will you go for something bold? What do you feel most confident and at ease in? Does it matter in terms of your audience? Will they expect professional attire or would they feel more at ease if you were wearing jeans and trainers? And don't forget footwear. You want to be comfortable and not run the risk of falling over during a particularly emphatic point.

Unfortunately you do have to consider your age and sex here. We know that older male speakers are often automatically taken more seriously in some contexts and assumed to have more expertise and authority on their subject area. They can often get away with looking more dishevelled and still be taken seriously. Younger speakers and women however often have to dress more smartly to gain respect. There are even articles written on not looking too feminine or even pinning your hair back if you have long hair. Apparently both, amongst some audiences, are associated with being taken less seriously. Amy has lost track of the number of times over the years that she has been told that 'she doesn't look like a professor' - meant as a compliment but one that sits uneasily with her. What does an expert look like?

These double standards are *absolutely* infuriating and unfair and it is up to you how you tackle it. As a new speaker you may want to err on the side of caution and then make more of a stance as your expertise gains reputation. Conversely that may sit uneasily with you. Only you can decide how you wish to play this and may make different decisions in different contexts.

As a final note you might want to check with the organisers beforehand what the set up will be and plan your clothing choices appropriately. A roving mic or headset will have a control box that needs to be held somewhere on your person. It is well known that many clothing designers seem to think that women do not need pockets on dresses which may leave only the strange experience of having to stuff the box into your bra. Not what you need if you're already nervous and have a burly sound engineer watching!

6. Engage with your audience

Encourage audience interaction - use your judgement here, but most audiences love to feel like you respect and value their expertise and opinion. A good way to involve them is to ask them to raise their hand if they've heard X, stand up if they are a nurse, sit down if they're vegetarian, raise both hands if they agree with Y, and so on. You need to use these tools with caution, as not only can they be irritating if over-used or used on the wrong audience, but you also need to allow time for the inevitable giggles, chatter and calm down after you do it.

Another important aspect of presenting is to connect with your audience. You don't just do this with witty anecdotes and self-deprecating humour. Make sure you look around the room when you speak, smile often, and make eye contact with several people (but never the same person all the time - that's just creepy!). It's also a really good idea to modulate your voice. This means varying the tone, pitch, tempo and volume of your voice so that you don't end up sounding monotonous. Don't be afraid to add emphasis to your words, leave the odd pregnant pause, or make your reactions obvious - it makes your message more captivating.

7. Know that audiences can vary

Finally, we'd be lying if we said that all presentation deliveries are the same. Sometimes you have an easy crowd who are inclined to naturally warm to you, and other times it's a tough gig and you leave the stage feeling unsure whether they appreciated what you had to say. This is just part and parcel of putting yourself out there. Sometimes you might get an uneasy feeling mid-presentation that your message isn't quite hitting the spot. When you feel like you're not connecting with the audience - read the room. If you have no laughs at stories that other audiences have found funny, it may be them, not you.

However, you can adapt your message if you don't feel it is working. Thankfully this doesn't happen often, but if you have a room full of stony faces and crossed arms, it's ok to take a pause and invite some interaction. Perhaps the talk isn't pitched quite at the right level - it's ok to poll the room and ask if they need you to give them more details, or more of the basics, so that the talk meets them where they are. Admittedly it is daunting to consider changing tack mid-talk, but sometimes this can save a presentation from falling flat on its face.

Sometimes a difficult or controversial topic can also be received like this. If you sense this is the problem, one thing we've learned over the years is that if you can't win their minds, try to win their hearts, and to some extent - vice versa. So, for example; sometimes you can get people to connect with your message by sharing a moving story, rather than facts (hearts). If they're not persuaded by the stories, try a hard-hitting fact that's difficult to argue with (minds).

One small point to think about here is the effect of any jokes or other engagement attempts, particularly if you are speaking in a country where they use simultaneous translation devices to translate your words into different languages. Due to the small time delay between you speaking, your words being translated, and your audience listening this can have the rather disconcerting effect of delayed reactions. The audience may all react at different times or you may have moved onto your next particularly unfunny point when the room breaks into laughter. Knowing to expect this can help not throw you off your train of thought.

8. Be kind to yourself

One little postscript we would add - you are likely to be your own worst critic. Be kind to yourself after your presentation. It's likely that *you* know the parts where you forgot your train of thought, or wish you'd phrased something differently, or your voice squeaked. We pretty much guarantee, everyone else will be far more generous than you are to yourself. Analysing every last detail of your presentation can be faintly exhausting. By all means look at any feedback gathered from the conference organisers, and use this to shape your work if it's useful, but do not sit and dissect your entire performance. You'll drive yourself nuts – and for no real benefit.

Also, remember that some people just like to whinge on the evaluation form or take the opportunity to tell you that they are better than you. Don't forget to look at the bigger feedback picture and all the positives you receive. Don't just zone in on the negative.

Developing your repertoire

Refreshing your material is important when you speak regularly. Not only do you need to update your presentations to ensure that they are full of current evidence-based information, but also you will probably want to expand your repertoire - this is important for when you get invited back for repeat presentations. The wider your talk portfolio, the more diversity you have as a speaker, and assuming you give the stellar presentation we know you can give, you'll be invited back.

If you can crack this one you might end up with a new conundrum. Some speakers are frequently requested, so their challenge is refreshing material so that there's always something new to offer. You know this yourself - there are probably speakers to whom you'd pay to listen time and time again right? You want to be like one of those, as opposed to a one-trick pony. Here are some good ways to keep those invites flowing:

- Develop different levels of detail for different audiences - beginner, intermediate and advanced. This is especially important if you speak to varied audiences. If you deliver your entry level talk to a group of people who are well versed in your subject, this will be embarrassing at best, and repetitive and uninteresting at worst. Equally, if you go straight in with a talk that only those with a Masters in the subject would understand, your talk will go over the heads of 90% of your audience. This is why it is so important to have a good working relationship with the conference organiser, so you can ask the level of understanding of the anticipated audience.

- Pick one small facet of your subject area, and plunder the existing knowledge on it. These 'deep-dive' talks can be truly fascinating, and to an invested audience who thinks they have 'heard it all', this can be a clever way to ensure that nobody is bored. They also appeal to a wide audience, because if you build your talk from the basic principles, and then expand and deepen the material within the talk, it will take the audience on a learning journey.
- Read around your subject widely, and learn to pick up on new developments that build on your work or book. You can set up alerts for journals, or make a habit of reading papers relevant to your subject matter. Keeping abreast of new research provides you with inspiration for refreshing your presentations.

One final administrative task you need to think about as you dip your toe deeper into the waters of speaking and presenting is managing your speaker portfolio. Scheduling talks, conferences, and managing the admin that comes with these can be a bit of a headache. Being organised will prevent a lot of frustration and wasted time. Saving your conference organiser time means you are much more likely to be invited back, as you are 'easy' to work with. Here is a selection of tips and time saving hacks:

- Create a talk catalogue - this is time intensive to begin with, but if you collate all your working talks, including the abstracts, objectives, and timings for them, as well as how to book you, what your charges are, and what other services you offer, you can simply send the catalogue to people who want you to speak for them.
- Remind people of what you speak about - you can do this on your website, via social media, by creating a newsletter, or with adverts.
- Have a section on your website where you clearly state your scope of expertise, and include recent talks, with reviews if possible.
- Have your CV up to date alongside abstracts, multiple choice questions (if required), reference lists, social media handles and pricing structures for your presentations ready so that you can send these off promptly.
- Publish feedback about your speaking engagements, or comments from the event organiser as testimonials.

Hopefully this chapter has inspired you to either think about putting yourself forward as a speaker, or developing your talks to improve your existing material. If you're still battling impostor syndrome or feeling of perfectionism, you may want to go back a few chapters to remind yourself of how awesome you are.

Chapter 16

Engaging with the media

It is possible that your work might attract some media attention. This might be more proactively through your publisher (or yourself) sharing a press release or more reactively in relation to news about your book spreading. Once your book is more widely read, or you have a reputation for being an expert on the subject area, reporters may come to you for interviews or supporting quotes for an article they are writing or in response to a media story.

The prospect of engaging with the media might make you excited or it might make you want to hide under the bed and never come out. The good news is that you do not have to do anything you do not want to do. You can turn down any offer you get. However, engaging with the media can be brilliant for your book publicity, particularly if you are savvy about what opportunities you choose to take. No two opportunities are likely to be the same, and it's absolutely fine to be all over one form / outlet and say a hard no to the others.

Types of media work you may get approached to do

There are different ways of sharing expertise via the media. You might be asked to give a supporting quote to a written piece, pre-record a statement or interview, or take part in a live interview on radio, television or social media. These different scenarios all require different skills and things to think about:

1. Providing a quote for a written piece

This is a common form of media request. Perhaps a journalist is writing a piece on your specialist topic, or even an issue that is in your book and would like you to add some supporting quotes. This can happen in a variety of ways. You might be asked to directly respond to set questions via email or perhaps you will have a phone conversation or video call with the reporter / magazine editor. The benefit of this approach is that you can ask to check over any final piece, or at least the quotes that you are attributed to within it. Don't forget to ask for this as the reporter may not always automatically send you the draft of the finished piece.

It might sound obvious, but remember that whatever you say or write down could be used as a quote. If you respond informally, your informal words could be used. If you are providing written quotes, take time over how you want those quotes to be phrased. Also, don't be afraid to add your own information if the questions posed don't include it. Some journalists will ask whether there is anything else you want to add, knowing they might have missed out some key questions. If they don't ask, you can add your own. Remember you can ask a friend or trusted colleague to read through before you send back

Always add or send details of where people can buy your book and ask for it to be added to the piece if at all possible. They may not be able to directly advertise where people can buy your book but they can refer to it in their text such as 'In her book 'Cat World Domination,' Joanna Blogs writes that...'.

2. Taking part in a pre-recorded interview

You might be asked to provide recorded quotes for a radio, television or social media production. Journalists may use all sorts of techniques for this including recording over the phone, via video messaging, recording live in person or in a studio, or even asking you to record voice notes and send them. The advice above applies here too. You can ask for the main questions or topics in advance so you can practice. You can ask to check the final quotes / recording. If you forget something or mumble your response you can ask to record again.

3. Taking part in a live interview on television and radio

This is probably the most daunting option for many people and you might want to think about building up to doing live interviews by getting more experience through written and pre-recorded quotes first. Saying that, a local radio station feature will probably feel less demanding than live national TV. Again, the advice above applies and a good journalist will most likely have a chat with you beforehand to a) explore your topic area and b) check that you can answer questions. Unless it is a major feature you will probably have very little time on air and it's a good idea to practise getting your key messages across in as few words as possible. More on this coming up.

Deciding whether to take a media opportunity or not

If you are approached to take part in a media piece you might want to take some time to think about it and then ask questions. This is a good idea when it is someone you haven't worked with before and are unsure about what their stance would be. It is a particularly good idea if the topic is controversial. Some key questions to think about include:

- What is the aim of the piece – why are you writing it?
- Will there be any particular adverts / promotion?
- Are you getting input from anybody else?
- If not live, will I see the final version before it goes out?
- Will I get any payment?
- Will there be an opportunity to share details of my work?
- If there is any negativity from the piece, who is responsible for that?

Another thing to think about is whether you are genuinely the best person for this opportunity. if it's an opportunity to talk directly about your work then, yes, of course you are! However, if it's a broader piece based on the subject of your work, or (as your reputation as being media friendly grows) something that's really not your expertise, then it's a good idea to stop and think about whether this is the right opportunity for you. What would help the piece more – your words or your silence? If you don't take part will they drop the piece or will they get someone else in? Is there someone inherently more qualified or experienced than you on this topic?

When deciding whether to take a media opportunity the BRAIN model can come in useful. This acronym stands for Benefits, Risks, Alternatives, Intuition and Nothing (as in doing nothing). You can do a quick BRAIN analysis of every media opportunity you get given.

Benefits

- Will this media piece potentially help others? Is it on a topic that is newsworthy and more people need information about?
- Will it help connect you to useful people? For example, who might be likely to read, hear or see the piece?
- Will it help develop your identity as an expert outside your inner circle and get you more widely known?

- Will this help develop your relationship with a journalist / presenter / magazine for any potential future opportunities?
- Are you being offered the opportunity instead of someone who might hold harmful views?

Risks

- Is there any chance of you being misconstrued deliberately, provocatively, or simply because there isn't enough time?
- Is it too far away from your specialist knowledge that you might come over as ill-informed?
- If it is a tricky topic, do you have the experience to navigate it?
- Are you being wheeled out as an expert when someone with more expertise (especially from an underrepresented group) is not?
- Is it on a topic that won't really benefit from this media attention, or worse, do harm?
- Do you risk becoming pigeonholed as 'that person who spoke about X on that programme'?
- Is it a waste of your overall time and resources compared to the benefits of taking part?

Alternatives

- Is there opportunity to provide comments in a different way?
- Can you say no to this opportunity but emphasise how open you are to further opportunities?
- Can you suggest someone else who might be better?
- Is there opportunity to change the topic or vary the approach?

Intuition

- What is your gut feeling about this opportunity? Where is that coming from? Is it nerves or your instinct telling you to avoid this?
- Have others had good or bad experiences with a similar topic?
- If you put out feelers to close trusted friends, what do they say?

Nothing

- What would happen if you simply said no to this opportunity?
- What would you gain or avoid by saying no? And what would you lose? What does the overall picture suggest?

Some tips for providing good quotes

Whichever form of media you have the option to do, there are some broad ground rules and advice that can help you make the most of the opportunity that you have been given.

1. Remember that your piece may be seen by a much broader audience than you usually write for or talk to

This means that people with differing experiences to your usual specific followers may be reading it. It's a good idea to think about what the opposition / reaction could be to your statements and think about how you might pre-empt that or soften your message. For example, you might be used to writing about the benefits of veganism to an audience who are typically vegans and supportive of your perspective. Put out the same statements in a national newspaper about the same thing and you will likely reach people who, shall we politely say, disagree with everything that you are saying.

Now it could be that you are so passionate about your message that you don't want to tone it down or adapt it to a broader audience. You might think any negativity is worth the specific message you want to get out there, or might indeed increase the reach of your piece. Alternatively, you might want to adapt your tone slightly adding in cautious words such as 'may' or 'could' or 'some' rather than make broad statements that sound like they apply to all.

Do also think about how your words could potentially upset or harm people outside of your usual circle. This is not to say that you should shy away from factual messages but it is unfair to be deliberately controversial to raise publicity at the risk of harming others.

Finally, keep your language simple. Remember that not everyone will have your in-depth subject knowledge. Do not use overly technical terms or feel that you have to present a highly scientific piece (unless you are on a highbrow scientific programme perhaps). Aim to make sure your message can be understood by as many people as possible.

2. Think about what you want your vibe to be

You've probably got a headshot and a short bio about yourself but make sure it's updated so you're ready to go with any media opportunities. Think about what you want to be called and described as. It can help to have a variety of headshots and ways of referring to yourself and describing your work prepared so that you can adapt them easily to the audience. You might want to use a different photo and description if you're writing some quotes for a tabloid newspaper than you might for a subject-specific magazine where people might know you better.

You want your audience to be able to relate to you. Describing yourself as a 'mum of two' might work brilliantly if you're writing for a parenting magazine but could get dismissed by a mainstream newspaper. Here, focussing on your qualifications and experience may be more appropriate. Having a photo of yourself clutching a knitted breast prop may work great for a breastfeeding specific magazine but not so much for the Daily Telegraph.

If you're being filmed, think about what you wear. Studios are so often designed for taller men wearing a shirt and trousers. If you're wearing a skirt or dress, think about the length and how you will perch on an uncomfortable stool that is probably designed for the average man's legs (and for someone wearing trousers).

Try also to make sure clothes aren't so eye-catching or distracting that people spend all their time wondering where you got your top or asking what on earth you are wearing (or worse). If you're filming from home, think about your camera angle and what's in the background. Hopefully the pandemic made us all a bit more savvy here, but it's worth a check.

Of course, you may want to do your bit about breaking down stereotypes by presenting yourself in the way you feel most authentic. Great. Just go into that with your eyes open and think about the balance between being yourself and moving your cause forward.

3. Decide what you want your message to be

It is likely that you will only have a few lines in an article or a few quotes broadcast for a radio or tv interview – although sometimes larger pieces are recorded. You need to make the most of that time. Think in terms of short memorable messages and sound bites / headlines. If you wanted to get your point across in one sentence, what would it be? Try to be as concise as possible. This isn't the place for swathes of detail, but rather the pertinent points.

Think about what messages would be most helpful to your audience? Unless you have lots of time, they don't need lots of background information. They need the take-home points – what is important to them? For example, if you are an academic talking about a piece of research, they don't need to know all the precise study methodology. They need to know simply what you did and what you found. Detail such as 'We conducted a survey with X and found...' is plenty. This isn't a conference presentation. Based on this, adapt your quotes to your audience, their interests and level of expertise.

For recorded pieces, if you know what the questions are likely to be beforehand take time to rehearse them. You can ask the journalist what they will ask; or if this opportunity hasn't arisen then make an educated guess about what they might be. You can write out your answers but try practising them out loud and speaking naturally. If it's really important that you get your words right you could write down answers and read them out but to be honest, you can usually tell when people are doing that as it sounds stilted.

Also, remember that people will recall what you said - not what you were asked. Reporters will want to ask the questions that suit them. Remember that your answers should suit you. You do not necessarily have to answer the direct question you were asked. You can avoid a part of it you don't want to answer or add in further information that you weren't asked, as long as you do this confidently, almost pretending that this is what you were asked.

4. Accept some things will be outside of your control

Although we would all love to have complete control over the article or piece we are quoted in, it is likely that some elements will be outside of your control. These are likely to include any accompanying photos or headlines. Often the journalist writes the piece and it is sent to an editor, or another staff member to write the headline which is typically designed to draw readers in. You can ask to see these, or make preferred suggestions, but you might need to accept they will not be considered. Sometimes even the journalist who wrote the piece has no say over the headline that is used.

Linked to this, some publications allow their articles to be freely reposted and shared on different sites as long as the authors and original source are included. Often unfortunately this does not include the article headline and you may find your work being shared on a different platform with an unhelpful or misleading one. It can be worth writing to the platform if this happens and sometimes they will change it. Sometimes however you just have to live with this risk.

Of course, it is likely that the publication you are writing for may differ in their response. A specialist magazine may be more likely to work closely with you on these elements whereas a mainstream newspaper may not. This may be another reason to start with smaller opportunities that you feel more confident in handling, rather than diving in at the deep end with a comment for a tabloid newspaper.

Once your piece is out there you also need to accept that you are not going to be able to control who shares it or what they say about it. 'Never read the comments' is good advice; that said, naturally you are immediately going to want to read the comments. It is also possible that an organisation or individual will share your article in a way that benefits them and again there is little you can do about this.

Our advice here is to work the possibility of this happening into your decision making. Is the overall piece still beneficial if it has a misleading headline or photo? Or is it not worth any potential negative outcomes? Again only you can make that decision.

What if it all goes wrong?

If you put yourself out there by doing media interviews, you need to consider the possibility that it could go wrong. You might stumble over your words, inadvertently say the wrong thing or be deliberately painted in an unhelpful way. Additionally, if your piece reaches a large audience there will most likely be some criticism however well you perform. Briefly here, as this is covered in depth in 'Dealing with criticism' (Chapter 17), remember that, much of the time, criticism is more about them than you and that some people simply like to troll from behind a keyboard. Focus on the positives and not the negatives, although we fully recognise that this can be very challenging, especially the first time it happens.

Overall, do your utmost to try not to be your own worst critic. Most people hate how they look and sound on recordings. Remember that unless you are super famous (or a member of parliament) you will remember whatever went wrong for far, far longer than anyone else will. Remind yourself of the old saying that 'today's news is tomorrow's chip paper'. Over time you will see that in the vast majority of cases this really is true and the world does move on.

If the worst happens, you have two main options in responding to a poor media piece:

1. Ignore and wait for it to go away. This can be a useful strategy when people are out to troll you or deliberately take offence at what you say. If you sense you can't win, move on. Don't take their bait.

2. Make a simple statement on your social media describing the situation. Make sure this is calm, factual and reiterates the points you want to make. Then it's usually best to ignore the comments.

Sometimes you might inadvertently say something that could be perceived to be critical or judgemental about a group of people, even if this is far from what you intended. In these cases a simple apology on social media stating that you were incorrect, that you did not intend to cause distress and recognising and apologising for any harm caused can go a long way. Don't preface it with a 'but' or an 'I'm sorry if anyone was upset by what I said' but make a simple and genuine apology.

Warnings aside, it's important to remember that most media opportunities go well, or are simply a short moment of fame. Do pick your opportunities carefully but they can be a brilliant way to build your profile and reach a larger audience. Good luck!

Chapter 17

How to handle criticism

Nobody likes to be criticised, particularly when it's over something really important to you. However, criticism is actually an important part of every author's career – a rite of passage as such. Whether it comes via email, social media, or the dreaded Amazon review, it means that you have made an impact on the world - even if it feels unfair or their comments are downright malicious.

Just like having a book proposal rejected, being criticised can bring up lots of negative emotions. Some might be directly related to their criticism of your book (how dare they criticise your baby!), whereas sometimes the broader experience of being criticised brings up self-doubts, impostor syndrome or past memories of being criticised. You might like to have a look back at the sections on dealing with rejection (Chapter five) or impostor syndrome (Chapter eight) to read in connection with this chapter.

Feeling angry, unsettled or upset by criticism is a normal reaction. It can be frustrating when criticism is unfair or inaccurate. It can be rage-inducing if you've written your book specifically to support others on a topic and the criticism is getting in the way of that or distorting your message. Naturally it can sting because criticism doesn't feel good. You've spent years of your life developing the knowledge and skills to write this book and now someone isn't being wholly appreciative of that? How dare they!

Receiving criticism is a good life lesson though, and not just specifically to writing. The Japanese proverb "Nana korobi, ya oki" - in other words "Fall down seven times, stand up eight" - is relevant here. Criticism is going to happen. At the risk of sounding cheesy, it's all about how you deal with criticism that matters. It's how you respond to, reflect on and act on that criticism that will determine whether it has a positive or negative impact upon your writing career.

If you struggle with criticism it can help to take a cold hard look at what is being said and reflect on what that means. Yes, criticism can hurt. But also, if you are being criticised it means that:

- Your book is being read and it is reaching those outside your inner circle who agree with you
- You are provoking opinion and discussion
- People care enough (for whatever reason) to criticise you
- You care enough about your book to read and react to criticism

That's much better than no one reading your book or caring enough to comment, right? Although it's brilliant to receive glowing praise, do you *really* only want to reach those who already agree with you? Isn't part of writing your book that people talk about its key issues and express their opinions about it? Isn't that how you change opinion, move things forward and make a real difference? Of course it is – but at the same time we do genuinely recognise how challenging this is (having been on the receiving end many times ourselves).

Why do people criticise books (or indeed anything)?

It's important to understand why people are criticising you as this can help shape both your response and how you feel about the criticism. Critics broadly fall into one of five categories. They are either:

- Genuinely curious, constructive and want to discuss. It's usually obvious who is trying to be helpful. They're probably more likely to contact you privately. Or also say something positive if they're responding publicly. We like these people and their feedback can be useful in helping improve out work.

- The people who are oblivious to what they don't know. This type of critic once had experience of something related to your book topic and is now obviously more of an expert than you. Or has a chip on their shoulder about 'experts'. Or had a different experience to your well researched book and you are therefore wrong. The Dunning-Kruger effect raises its head again here.

- The person who wants to put down your work in order to promote themselves. These are the sorts of critics who post things like *'oh wow, look how awful this person's work is. I can't believe she said that. If you want to learn more about the correct way to think about this, join me on my new course'*.

- The person who is triggered by what you have written. We know that people can carry a lot of grief and trauma around with them due to their life experiences. Sometimes what you write, no matter how evidence based or factual, can trigger that for them. This is going to be dependent on the subject area. For example, if you are writing a book about how to fix a boat engine, this is probably going to get less of an emotional response than if you are writing about babies or a health problem - unless you find people with particularly bad experiences of fixing boat engines!
- Trolls who just enjoy being nasty or are trying to derail your time. Their thrill is in getting a rise from you and seeing that you cared enough to respond. They enjoy causing chaos or trying to goad you into a non-professional response.

The easy accessibility of the internet today has made criticism more common, both in terms of accessibility and speed. Yes, years ago if you were disgruntled about a book you had read you could write in to a newspaper, or ring up the local radio and share your displeasure. Maybe you moaned at your book club (if you had progressed past the wine to actually reading the book!). Or told your friends about it over dinner. What you didn't tend to do was shout your criticism into the universe for all to hear – or in other words, post it on the internet.

The internet also amplifies the voices of the critics and the critical. Whereas before if one in one hundred people didn't like your book but the rest loved it, you'd be far more likely to come into contact with positive feedback and rarely, if ever, meet the people who disliked it. Now, people find others just like them with such ease on the internet that it can seem like rare shared experiences (such as disliking your book) are more common than they are. If these people then group together and start discussing (or tweeting nastiness at you and about you) then it gives the false impression of them being a much bigger contingent than they are. Disgruntled people tend to protest loudly whereas many people who really quite enjoyed your book just got on with their lives.

Unfortunately, the rise of accessible information on the internet has also made people think they are far more expert than they actually are. Some people think that because they can instantly search for something on their phone then they know everything there is to know on said subject. They fail to see all your years of expertise, training and researching and instead somehow think their quick internet search equates to (or trumps) your expertise. We bet these people also tell the mechanic at the garage just what is wrong with their car / query why it is taking so long. They may well find one research paper online and declare it 'the truth', but as the expert in the subject you will know its limitations, real findings (rather than the abstract they just read) and how it fits with all the hundreds, even thousands, of other papers on the topic. Remember you are the expert (and have a look back at the impostor syndrome chapter if you are wavering).

Choose whose feedback you listen to

The greater the reach of your work, the more likely it is that you will receive criticism. It would be easy to say, 'Oh don't listen to any of it, they're just jealous / bored / evil.' That will of course apply to some criticism that you receive (much of it in fact). Nevertheless it's highly unlikely that your book will be totally free of justified criticism. No book is perfect. No expert is perfect. No writer is perfect. We include established authors in that too. Both of us can reel off a list of what we'd go back and change in hindsight (or in future editions) of our books.

The important part is whose judgement you decide to listen to. Whose opinion matters to you? Who do you respect enough to criticise you? Who do you trust enough to take advice from? Who is important enough to you that you will spend precious time listening and possibly feeling deflated over? This is the perfect time to draw on the work of the brilliant Professor Brene Brown around criticism, shame and belonging.

Firstly, in her book Daring Greatly she talks about how she carries a small piece of paper in her wallet with the names of people whose opinion actually matters to her. If you're not on that list you're not getting into Brene's head. Who would be on your list? Your partner perhaps, or children? Your publisher and editor? Collaborators? You get to choose the list but be strict. Yes there will likely be some work / writing peers on there and maybe a big shot you're trying to impress in your field. But if everything fell apart tomorrow, who would be there for you? It's *those* people who should really be on that piece of paper.

The good thing about the people on your bit of paper is that they probably do criticism well. It is constructive and kind and not about trying to bring you down. This is where criticism can be a great learning opportunity - it helps us to grow as writers, develop new skills and keep moving forward. Listen to what they are saying and take time to consider whether they are right. It's ok to put some distance in between any feedback and this reflection.

You might want to go back and read the section on book proposals and rejection again here. Always remember that constructive criticism is not a judgement of you as a person. It doesn't mean that you're a terrible writer and all the things in your book are wrong. It also doesn't mean that you're a useless person/ unsuccessful/ will never be a skilled writer.

Sometimes useful criticism gets communicated in an unhelpful way. Anonymous reviews can be particularly stinging sometimes as people forget that there is a person and a whole lot of effort behind the screen. Try to focus on the core points that are made - such as your book could benefit from a few diagrams - rather than the *'useless book, a complete waste of my time and money'* style padding.

Of course this means that there are lots of people whose opinions you don't need to worry very much about. This links neatly into a second great quote from Brene in relation to who *wouldn't* be on that list. In a brilliant video entitled 'Why Your Critics Don't Count' [available on YouTube][7] she refers to a famous quote by Thomas Roosevelt[8]:

> *"It is not the critic who counts; not the man who points out how the strong man stumbles, or where the doer of deeds could have done them better. The credit belongs to the man who is actually in the arena, whose face is marred by dust and sweat and blood; who strives valiantly; who errs, who comes short again and again, because there is no effort without error and shortcoming; but who does actually strive to do the deeds; who knows great enthusiasms, the great devotions; who spends himself in a worthy cause; who at the best knows in the end the triumph of high achievement, and who at the worst, if he fails, at least fails while daring greatly, so that his place shall never be with those cold and timid souls who neither know victory nor defeat."*

7 https://brenebrown.com/videos/99u-why-your-critics-arent-the-ones-who-count/

8 https://www.goodreads.com/quotes/7-it-is-not-the-critic-who-counts-not-the-man

In relation to this Brene simply says, *'If you're not in the arena getting your ass kicked I'm not interested in your feedback.'* This says it all. Many of your less constructive critics will not be an expert on your topic area, will not have written a book, and will not be out there promoting it. Why are you giving so much energy to what they think?

Is it because you think that 'bOOkCrITiC10345' with a cartoon avatar for a profile picture really knows better than you on the topic? Or is it because the experience of being criticised is pushing those buttons of yours that remind you of the time you failed at something / were told you weren't good enough by someone you loved / were shamed in front of others? Stop giving some random person on the internet equal credit for understanding your expert subject area as well as you do. Finally and most certainly, *do not* let them have so much power over your emotions and perceptions of success.

Some tips for dealing with unconstructive critics

Working on the basis that not all criticism is going to be helpful, and that it can feel pretty demoralising to be on the receiving end of it, here are some tips for moving past it:

- Realise that these things are usually about the critic and not actually anything to do with you. People criticise you because you have triggered something in them with your work. Maybe it's on a topic that brings up bad memories or trauma for them. Maybe you make them feel jealous, inadequate or guilty that they are not achieving what they want to achieve. Maybe they are just really overwhelmed and stressed. None of these are anything to do with the quality of your work or you as a person.

- Have some trusted friends that you can confidentially vent to about people's ridiculous criticism. You might want a mix of people here. Generally, when we have a problem we are either looking for solutions, or to vent, or someone to listen (or sometimes all of these). So have some friends who will be tactful and kindly and openly point out where criticism might be constructive and useful. But also have some who will be furious on your behalf and donate noisy toys to your critics' children!

- Write out a response to your critics, pointing out how ridiculous they are and just where they can get off. Do not post this or send it. We repeat - *do not* post this or send it. Sometimes the act of just typing it out helps you process some of the rage.

- Remind yourself of the bigger picture. When atrocities happen, we are reminded to look to the good people or the 'helpers'. Not to put your bad review on the same level as a terrorist attack, but the same principle applies here. Often it is far too easy to focus on the minority of bad reviews than it is on all the good things people say. When you are feeling down, remind yourself of the good stuff.

- It can help to reflect on why you are feeling this way. Is it just anger that someone has criticised something you know is well written? Is it anger that they are derailing an important conversation, particularly if you have written your book to try and help others? Or is it that they are poking old wounds that you carry about your self-worth? If it's the latter it might be worth thinking about some life coaching or counselling to help you process these thoughts.

- Imagine that your good friend had written the book and comes to you upset about this criticism. What would you say to them? Placing this distance between your book and your reaction helps you a) see the strength of your book without any associated subconscious feelings that you're not good enough and b) allows you to respond with the kindness that you reserve for others.

- If you do end up in a situation where you need to respond to a criticism publicly, such as during a presentation or debate, it can help to take a magnanimous approach or to 'kill them with kindness'. Depending on their behaviour it can help to keep repeating to yourself the words of Michelle Obama here 'When they go low, we go high'. People will remember your reaction.

- Share with good humour some of the more ludicrous reviews. This could be with close friends over a coffee. Or if they are anonymous, sometimes sharing ridiculous reviewers in a good-natured way can help other writers too. It can show people that everyone gets crazy reviewers sometimes. Keep it light hearted and directed at the review content, not the reviewer themselves though.

- Remember that if you do respond to critics who are disingenuous then it's going to be an almighty time drain. They will be thrilled you have responded and see this as encouragement to keep going. Remind yourself that you are saving time by just walking away. Not that we make a particular daily habit of quoting Winston Churchill, but his famous saying *'You will never reach your destination if you stop and throw stones at every dog that barks'* is apt here. Don't let them waste your time. Remember that words written in emails and on social media can last forever.

- On this note beware of sea lions! 'Sea lioning' is a more subtle and irritating form of trolling with the aims of wasting your time, trying to make you look unreasonable and slowly driving you insane. Sea lions appear initially to be asking polite questions. You post something on social media and the sea lions will turn up with their questions. No matter what you respond with, they have more questions. And after that more questions. And requests for further information and evidence (which is often easily Google-able). They get their name from the sea lion who barks over and over.

- Most of all, take the opportunity to learn from criticism, whether that's from its content, how you present and disseminate your work, or in terms of your own personal vulnerabilities and weaknesses.

Finally, always remember that you're probably your own worst critic. Be as kind to yourself as you would a friend. After all, you've written a book – you're a Rockstar.

Chapter 18

What next?

We've taken you through the why and how of writing a book, who you are as a writer, and what possible areas for improvement you might have. Hopefully you are now feeling more informed and confident, but sometimes making a start is the most daunting part. Having made it all the way to the end of this book, you may be wondering, 'what next?'

We've said this already - writing is a journey. At some point you will need to strike out and start somewhere. Exactly where you are on the spectrum of writing progress will obviously dictate where that starting point is and what your first steps will be.

Whether you are contemplating your first or fifth book, we find that making a writing plan can help get the thoughts out of your head and down on paper. This isn't about starting to write the actual words in your book and is different to a book structure. Instead it is a strategy to brainstorm what your book will look like, who your target audience (and publishers) might be, and what skills you might need to take you to the next step of starting writing.

You might already have notes jotted down somewhere but if not, we have brought together some of the key elements of planning your book in the table on the next page. Even if you don't have the time to begin writing your book right now, getting your thoughts organised on paper can feel very cathartic. Creating a logical plan can help a hugely overwhelming task to feel more manageable and enable you to make a start. It also feels very satisfying to see a plan written down on paper!

Your writing action plan

Areas to consider	Ideas	Resources	Timescale
Book genre			
Working title			
Structure / chapters			
What do I want to achieve with my book?			
Target audience			
Competing works			
Publishing options			
What strengths do I already have?			
What do I need to get better at?			
What support do I need?			

The book genre is probably the easiest place to start. You will almost certainly know this immediately but it is still important to define it especially if you will be pitching your book to an agent or publisher.

Your working title can be helpful for you to begin thinking about early. It can take a surprisingly long time to think of a title that you feel happy with. The title needs to help your reader identify that this book meets their needs, and piques their interest. You can always change the title if your book ends up taking a different direction as it comes together.

In terms of structure, when you begin to think about your book it may be obvious what your chapters will need to cover. At the planning stage, this could be as simple as coming up with a purpose or aim for each chapter. The chapter outline can also help you to identify how many chapters you are likely to include and the approximate word count. This may be helpful for your publisher, but also helps you to think about how you will compose and set down the chapter.

An important aspect to think about is **what you want your book to achieve**. Reflecting back on the 'why write' sections in this book you may have many personal reasons for writing. Nevertheless what do you want your book to mean for others? What knowledge do you want to expand in others? How do you want your readers to feel? What changes would you like to see following the publication of your work? The answers to these questions may help you shape your chapters, title and even possibly expand your audience.

The next aspect to consider is your **target audience**. This needs to be absolutely clear in your mind from the word go. Your intended audience may greatly influence the style of your writing, and how much evidence will be needed, so be as specific as possible. There are more tips about this in Chapter three.

It is never too early to think about **competing works**, to ensure your book is unique enough, to avoid plagiarism and develop a distinctly different book from those currently available. Start by looking for books on your topic - and consider their titles, popularity (check the competing books' Amazon rankings), price and target market. Think about and write down what makes yours different.

You may already have a **dream publisher** in mind, but consider whether you are prepared to be flexible on this. Will you approach the publisher directly, or will you be seeking representation from a literary agent. You'll find more about this in Chapters four and five.

We always think it's a good idea when planning a book to **make a note of the strengths that you do have**. Too often as writers we focus on our critics or our perceived limitations without taking the time to remember the strengths and experiences we have that led us to want to write this book in the first place. As well as boosting your confidence, this does also help keep your expertise in the forefront of your mind when it comes to shaping and promoting your book to publishers, promoters and readers.

In terms of whether there is **anything you need to improve**, you may feel entirely ready and qualified to begin your book, or you may immediately know what to prioritise. There may be areas that are important for your book, but require a brief literature search before you go any further. Perhaps you need to speak to a specialist, develop your writing skills, or maybe work on your self-doubt and impostor syndrome. We have lots of resources you can access in terms of writing clubs and mentorship, or perhaps you need something specific.

Finally, take a moment to think about what **support you could draw on from others**. This might be a chat with your partner about what you will need in terms of space and time to write your book. You might need to think about childcare plans or calling in some favours from friends. Or maybe you'll think about some time limited expenditure like a meal preparation service or cleaner if this is in your budget. We are certainly not saying that you have to have these things in place to write a book, but that they can really help in supporting your writing if you do have the privilege of being able to access them. If you are struggling for money or support you might have to be a bit more creative - but remember, prioritising yourself and your writing is not selfish. It deserves investment, even if that's simply an additional supply of your favourite chocolates to bribe yourself through the tricky bits.

As you begin to fill in this table, you will basically develop your own bespoke action plan. It may be that as you complete it, your thoughts begin to take shape and you feel the thrill of the book forming a tangible outline in your head. If this happens, ride the wave of your imagination and write down everything you can think of. Some people choose to create a mind map, others just simply note down everything that springs to mind. Don't worry about the order and logic too much - just get it down. You can reorder sections or delete anything irrelevant later. Many people find that the introduction chapter is the very last thing that they write. Don't let it act as a barrier to getting the rest of the book done! If inspiration does hit, you might like to start thinking about the macrostructure of your book:

- The overarching purpose of your book, and the point you are trying to make
- How you will guide your reader through that thought process
- Chapter structure, flow and order
- Possible word count for each chapter
- An approximate timeline for completing each chapter

Once you have this macrostructure fleshed out, you could begin to think about what content you will have in each chapter. Then you 'simply' have to fill that structure in! Remember that beginning a book is often the hardest part, and the task that many often worry most over. This is why beginning to write anything at all is often a good plan. Starting somewhere, anywhere seems to move an author from the stagnant position of 'I Can't' to 'I Am'. Remember that even if you only write 500 words a day, or even a week, eventually you will have something that is starting to resemble a draft manuscript.

Hopefully you're now fired up, filled with enthusiasm and nervous excitement for what your book may bring. Whether you write one or twenty books, our hope is that you are now equipped with the knowledge and information you need to write the high quality book we know you're capable of.

We wish you the very best of luck.

Index

Printed in Great Britain
by Amazon

78702603R00122